LON

BEST

Bed & Breakfast

HOTELS

Clean, Safe and Friendly
Bed and Breakfast Hotels
in Central and Outer London

Inspected and Recommended by

MARY BISHOP & SUSAN YARDLEIGH

London's Best Bed & Breakfast Hotels 1990-91 Edition © FHG Publications
ISBN 1 85055 122 7
Hotel Descriptions © Mary Bishop, Susan Yardleigh

Typeset by RD Composition Ltd., Glasgow.
Printed and bound by Benham's Ltd., Colchester.

Published by FHG Publications Ltd., a member of the U.N. Group.
Abbey Mill Business Centre, Seedhill, Paisley PA1 1JN (041-887 0428).

Distributed by John Bartholomew & Son Ltd., PO Box Glasgow (041-772 3200).

US ISBN 1-55650-225-7
Distributed in the United States by
Hunter Publishing Inc., 300 Raritan Center Parkway CN94, Edison, N.J., 08818, USA

Contents

INTRODUCTION   4   HOW TO USE THIS GUIDE   10

Maps: *Central London*   13
        Outer London   75

CENTRAL LONDON ACCOMMODATION

Bayswater	14
Bloomsbury	17
Chelsea and Sloane Square	28
Covent Garden	30
Earls Court	34
Kensington High Street	38
Knightsbridge and South Kensington	41
Marylebone and Marble Arch	46
Notting Hill and Holland Park	52
Paddington	55
Soho	63
Victoria	65

OUTER LONDON ACCOMMODATION

Chiswick	76
Clapham	80
Ealing	81
Eltham	83
Hampstead and Golders Green	86
Harrow	89
Ilford and Forest Gate	92
Kew and Richmond	95
Kingston upon Thames	97
Swiss Cottage	99
Theydon Bois	100
Wimbledon	101
Gatwick Airport (Horley)	102
Heathrow Airport (Hayes and Hounslow)	106

SPECIAL REQUIREMENTS

Disabled Visitors	108
Children	108
Dogs Welcome	109
Parking Available	109

INDEX   110

Publisher's Note

MAPS. The maps in *London's Best Bed & Breakfast Hotels* will give readers an indication of where places are – but since they are largely diagrammatic they cannot be precise or detailed.

We strongly recommend that readers use one of the easily available and inexpensive London Street Guides or Maps obtainable in bookstalls, kiosks and bookshops from such publishers as Geographer's A-Z, Yellow Pages, Geographia, Bartholomew's and Robert Nicholson. Maps are also available from the London Tourist Board and London Transport.

ACKNOWLEDGEMENTS. The authors and publishers are grateful to the managers and owners of the many establishments visited without warning during the preparation of this guide. We also thank: London Transport for the Underground Map on our cover. Picturebank Photo Library Ltd. for Tower Bridge and Big Ben on the front cover. Tom Murphy for diagram/maps. Ted Carden for layout and cover design. Advertisers for their support.

DISCLAIMER. All information is given here in good faith but the authors and publishers regret that they cannot accept responsibility for errors, omissions or misrepresentations in our entries or any consequences thereof.

Readers should check prices and other terms before booking.

Authors' Foreword

All the establishments listed and described in this guide have been visited by ourselves and selected solely for their suitability for you, the visitor.

None has paid or been asked to pay for their entry.

Some have taken paid advertising space as an extra promotion and this is displayed quite separately from the standard descriptive entries. These entries have been written and are presented here without the previous involvement of proprietors, managers or their staff.

We wish you all a very happy stay in London!

Mary Bishop
Susan Yardleigh

Introduction

The Aim of this Guide

"London's Best Bed and Breakfast Guide" was originally launched to fill an enormous gap in the market. Before then there was no guide devoted exclusively to London's B&B's. Considering that London welcomes some 24 million visitors a year, the existing guides were unable, due to space restrictions, to provide enough detail on London's B&B's. Most guides either cover the whole country or embrace too broad a spectrum of London's range of accommodation – hotels, hostels and apartments as well as B&B's. Thousands of visitors to London do not have the means to stay at expensive hotels and had great difficulty in gaining advance information on cheaper forms of accommodation. Happily, however, since the appearance of *London's Best Bed and Breakfast Hotels* many of these visitors have been able to find a B&B that is just right for them and with the addition of several new areas, we hope this new edition will be even more successful.

This guide also addresses itself to those who are weary of the uniformity and impersonal character of so many present-day chain hotels, and who long for the simplicity of a smaller establishment. Note that some of our more expensive B&B's (those in the region of £55-£70) offer accommodation that is as luxurious and far more charming than that of many three and four star hotels.

The condition of individual Bed and Breakfast establishments in London varies tremendously. Sadly, there are many which are dirty and run-down and there are many which now house homeless families and tramps. Our second aim in writing this book therefore is to help you, the visitor, to avoid such establishments. Time and again they have spoiled the holidays of unsuspecting tourists in London.

Of all the B&B's we inspected, less than a third came up to the standards we set.

Our Standards for Inspection

Breaking away from the patterns of traditional guide books, which often place more emphasis on a wide range of *facilities* (e.g. bar, bedside tables, trouser presses, etc.) than on the *quality* of an establishment, we have decided to apply only *three* criteria; the three which we feel to be of greater importance than any others. These are:

1)   **CLEANLINESS**

2)   **ATMOSPHERE**. A combination of friendly, helpful staff and inviting premises.

3)   **VALUE FOR MONEY**. Generally reasonable, but we have included a few B&B's whose prices are a little on the high side. This is purely because they are outstanding in all other aspects and often offer one or two "extras".

What is a London "Bed and Breakfast"?

First and foremost, a London B&B is not necessarily a hotel, despite the fact that many use the word in their name. There is seldom a lift (elevator) and rooms can be as high as the 5th floor. Generally bedrooms are on the small side. They are invariably far smaller than their equivalents in North America or Australia for example, and you will find that some rooms do not have electricity sockets! Very few have formal restaurants: normally breakfast is the only meal of the day which they offer. There is no room service (though many now provide tea and coffee making facilities), and in many establishments the Reception is no more than a corner of the breakfast room or an area little more than a metre square under the stairs!

None is purpose-built, most being conversions of 18th and 19th century houses constructed in the days when families had many children and as many servants. Anyone who has watched the TV series "Upstairs – Downstairs" will recognise this type of house, many of which retain their lovely moulded ceilings, elegant staircases and even original fireplaces. The latter are sadly no longer used, as London is now a smokeless zone and such fires are forbidden. Readers, fear not! All the B&B's listed in this book have either central or some other form of heating to protect you from our winter climate!

London B&B's are quite different from most of those in other parts of Britain. They are run on serious business lines (as opposed to being a supplementary source of a family's income in the country) and some of the cheaper ones, therefore, tend to be plain and functional rather than charming. Note that, because of the scarcity of accommodation and high rates in London, they are also somewhat more expensive than their country counterparts.

Owners, Managers and Staff

London is a cosmopolitan city and it is one of its delights that the B&B's, like the restaurants, are owned and run by people from many different lands, e.g. from Italy, Spain, Yugoslavia, Cyprus, Poland, etc. Only a few London B&B's are actually run by English people, surprising though it may sound!

There is one thing, however, which the London B&B's listed in this guide do have in common with their country sisters and that is their *warm welcome*. We have found the managers and staff of all these establishments to be most friendly and helpful – they will take a personal interest in your visit and will be happy to give you tips on sightseeing. They'll direct you to the nearest bank, advise you on good local restaurants and generally make your stay as enjoyable as possible.

Choosing the Area to Suit your Needs

One of the first things to decide is where, in this vast city, you wish to stay. We have therefore included maps of both Central and Outer London and a brief "Pen Portrait" of the different areas to help readers decide which one most suits their particular needs and priorities. It has often been said that London is a collection of villages, and this was, indeed, the way the city came into being. This also accounts for the diversity of character and architectural styles. Because, understandably, many visitors wish to be in the centre, particularly if their visit is a short one, we have included the maximum number of B&B's there. However, a twenty- or thirty-minute Underground journey can be well worthwhile if it leads to a place of charm and character where the air is sweeter, where the restaurants are better as well as cheaper and where local pubs are real "Locals" and not simply tourist haunts. We have therefore included B&B's in a number of the better areas outside the centre and also in the neighbourhood of the two main arrival airports – Gatwick and Heathrow. See section 3.

Safety First! No Need to Worry

All areas covered by this book are usually safe and pleasant. B&B's in the "Central London" section are all within a 10 minute walk of the nearest tube station. Those which are located in the "Outer London" section or in the "Airports" section are often very near a tube station. If this is not the case, access will be via bus or British Rail. Since detailed travel instructions are included with all entries, you should have no difficulty in finding the establishment of your choice.

Transport in London

UNDERGROUND AND BUSES

The "Tube" (as the London Underground is known) and the red London Transport schedule buses run from approximately 5.45 a.m. to 12.00 midnight Mondays to Saturdays and 7.45 a.m. to 11.00 p.m. (2300) on Sundays. Night buses run approximately half-hourly services on most major routes throughout the night, every day of the week. Note that buses and tubes become very crowded during the rush hours – Monday to Friday 7.30-10.00 a.m. and 4.00 p.m. (1600) to 6.30 p.m. (1830). Avoid travelling at those times if you can, for your own comfort.

Airbuses run from Heathrow Airport to Central London every twenty minutes, from approx. 6.30 a.m. to 9.30 p.m. (2130) daily.

Daily passes or travelcards for the buses and the tubes are available. These are valid after 9.30 a.m. weekdays and all day at the weekend at a minimal cost of £2.30 to cover both services. If you are staying in London for four or more days you should purchase some sort of weekly pass or travelcard. These work on a basis of zones and cost approx. £7.10 for the Centre Zone, for example. You can find out about these from any Underground station, also from British Rail stations and many news-agents. For further information, phone London Regional Transport on 071-222 1234.

Cars

For those thinking of coming to London by car, we strongly advise finding a B&B with parking (see Special Requirements section, p. 109), then using public transport to get around. To drive or park a car in Central London (except on Sundays) can be quite a nightmare for a resident, let alone a visitor!

How to Use this Guide

The book is divided into three sections. The first is for *Central London* (as defined by London Transport Travelcard Zone 1), the second is for *Outer London* and the third is for the main *Airports* – Gatwick and Heathrow.

These sections are sub-divided into areas with the B&B's listed alphabetically within each area. At the back of the book you will find lists for those with special needs – facilities for children, disabled, dogs and car parking and an index of all the establishments included.

Prices

We have sought to avoid the complicated symbols used in most guide books, retaining only one (£) to indicate the rates you may expect to pay. These are indicated thus:

£	Up to £32 Double/Twin Room
	Up to £22 Single Room
££	£33–£45 Double/Twin Room
	£23–£30 Single Room
£££	£46–£55 Double/Twin Room
	£31–£40 Single Room
££££	£56–£70 Double/Twin Room
	£41–£55 Single Room

(*Note:* Double = 1 large bed, Twin = 2 single beds)

These prices can, naturally, only form a general guideline, since they are subject to seasonal variations. **Always confirm prices when making a booking, and check that they include breakfast, VAT (tax) and service charges.** We have not included prices for three, four or five-bedded rooms, but you will find that the rate per person will be lower than in a single or double room – a useful hint for families or small groups travelling on a budget.

Reservations

Every entry has full details of address and telephone number so that you can book directly by phone or letter.

It is always wise to reserve at least six weeks in advance. The exceptionally busy periods are normally Easter, July, September and October. If at all possible, make a provisional reservation by telephone (if not, then in writing, as follows), backing up your call with a letter stating clearly the type of room you wish to reserve, the date and the time of arrival and the number of nights you wish to stay. If there are children in the party or if it is a weekend, ask if any special reductions are available. A deposit will normally be required and you can enclose this in the form of a cheque (International Money Order or Eurocheque if writing from abroad) usually to cover the first night's accommodation. Mention any special requirements, e.g. ground-floor room or baby's cot, and ask for a receipt and letter of confirmation.

In Case of Difficulty

If you have difficulty in finding accommodation, make your way to one of the offices of the London Tourist Board listed below. For a small fee, their friendly, multi-lingual staff will be able to arrange accommodation and also help you with any other enquiries regarding sightseeing tours, theatre tickets, etc.

LONDON TOURIST BOARD

Main Office: Victoria Station Forecourt, London SW1

Other Offices: Harrods (*Basement*), Brompton Road, SW1
Tower of London (*summer only*)
Selfridges, Oxford Street, W1 (*basement*)
Heathrow Airport (*Underground entrance for Terminals 1, 2 and 3*)

Tourist Information: *Telephone* (071)-730 3488

Complaints

We very much hope that you will be happy with the B&B you choose from this guide. However, should you have any cause for complaint or suggestions for improvement, please do not hesitate to pass them on to the owner or manager, who will usually be only too keen to put things right.

If you have a serious complaint which cannot be settled on the spot, you should contact the London Tourist Board (071-730 3450) and you should also write to us. We will follow up all such complaints but we regret that we cannot act as intermediaries or on your behalf nor can we or the Publishers accept responsibility for any of the services or accommodation described.

All the establishments described are recommended in good faith but they can change hands or staff and other problems can arise which result in a deterioration of standards. In such cases neither the authors nor the Publishers can be held responsible.

Cancellations

Remember that a confirmed booking is a form of legal contract. The proprietor has obligations to you and you also have to keep the bargain. Always give as much notice as possible if you have to cancel or leave early. If the accommodation is not re-let, the proprietor may be within his rights in retaining any deposit and even requesting additional payment.

Invitation to Readers

The authors and Publishers are always keen to hear visitors' comments on the establishments listed in this guide. We also welcome reports on any good B&B's which may have escaped our attention. If you have any good news to pass on, please contact us through **FHG Publications Ltd., Abbey Mill Business Centre, Seedhill, Paisley PA1 1JN.**

1 Bayswater
2 Bloomsbury
3 Chelsea & Sloane Square
4 Covent Garden
5 Earls Court
6 Kensington High Street
7 Knightsbridge & S. Kensington
8 Marylebone & Marble Arch
9 Notting Hill & Holland Park
10 Paddington
11 Soho
12 Victoria

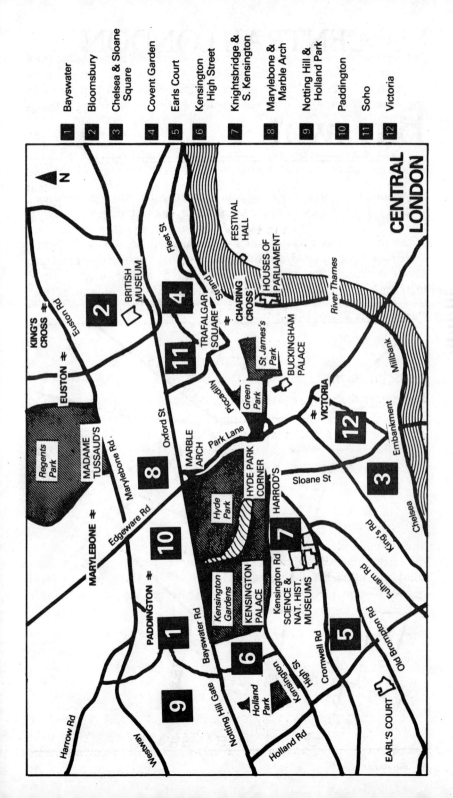

CENTRAL LONDON

Bayswater

Bayswater lies north of Kensington Gardens, the more "manicured" section of Hyde Park west of the Long Water. In the south-west corner of these 275 acres of parkland is situated Kensington Palace, known to many of the royal family who have their London home here as "KP" (some State rooms and Court-dress collection open to the public: charge). Here also is the Round Pond where in times gone by nannies used to wheel their charges. These days one is more likely to see local people airing their

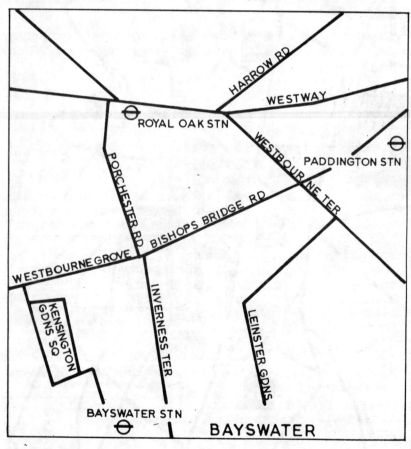

dogs, or young footballers practising their game, while at week-ends the model boat enthusiasts take over.

Facing the gardens are some of London's most attractive large hotels, notably Whites and Park Court with their elegant facades and, further west, the London Embassy. It makes a pleasant start to the evening to sip a cocktail or two here in the attractive bar which opens, in summer, onto a large terrace, especially during Happy Hour – half-price time! Alongside runs Bayswater's most charming street: St. Petersburgh Place, its name reflecting the former Russian influence in this part of London although the three places of worship that remain are Anglican, Greek Orthodox and Jewish. Beautiful houses with equally beautiful gardens also line the street. However Bayswater, like so many in London, is an area of contrasts: Queensway, which bisects it, is cosmopolitan and scruffy as are many of the surrounding streets and squares and only a few good B&B's are left.

Restaurants in and around Queensway are, like Paddington, cheap and cheerful but there are some good Greek ones around and for lovers of Indian food, Westbourne Grove is said to have the best selection in London.

Transport facilities are excellent: lots of buses and two underground stations – Bayswater (Circle and District lines) and Queensway (Central line).

Places to Visit

Kensington Gardens	Portobello Road Market
Kensington Palace	Serpentine Gallery
London Toy and Model Museum	Shakespeare Globe Museum

Garden Court ═══════

30 Kensington Garden Square
London
W2 4BG   Tel 071-727 8304

Price Band	£–££
Credit Cards	None
Bathrooms	Private and shared
Television	In lounge
Breakfast	English
Telephone	Public
Parking	Difficult

Although the area in which it is situated has become a little rundown recently, this long-established budget B&B has always kept its standards.

Many bedrooms face the Square and are light, airy and spotless, though simple as is the breakfast room. On the ground floor is a lounge for TV viewing which doubles as a bar which is a cosy place to discuss the day's sightseeing with other visitors or with the very friendly staff.

During 1989 the two top floors have been imaginatively refurbished and the owner plans to do the whole hotel over the next two years or so. For the moment, however, the extra climb is well worthwhile.

Travel Instructions: *Underground to Bayswater. Turn left on leaving the station and take the second left which is Porchester Gardens and leads into Kensington Garden Square – Garden Court is on the other side of the square.*

The Royal Oak ═══════════

88 Bishops Bridge Road
London
W2 5AA   Tel 071-229 2886

Price Band	£–££
Credit Cards	Access, Visa
Bathrooms	Shared
Television	In some rooms
Breakfast	Continental
Telephone	Public
Parking	Difficult

The Royal Oak is something quite unusual for London – a pub which offers top-class accommodation. The bedrooms were all refurbished recently and are most attractive. Russet-coloured carpets blend with deep orange cotton bedspreads. The furniture is of light pine and the rooms are more spacious and airy than most in London. There are tea and coffee making facilities in all rooms.

The Royal Oak is also unusual with respect to its charges. If one pays on a nightly basis prices are just a little on the high side. However, if one stays seven nights, one only pays for four, which makes it more or less the cheapest B&B in central London! Highly recommended for long stays.

Travel Instructions: *Underground to Bayswater. Turn left out of the station and walk to the end of Queensway. You will see the Royal Oak on the opposite side of the road (5 minutes' walk).*

Bloomsbury

Bloomsbury, the area just east of Tottenham Court Road, is what our Japanese visitors would call a "safety area". It is leafy, elegant and respectable. Noted for its squares – Russell, Bedford, Tavistock – most of which are surrounded by fine 18th century houses once occupied by single families but now mainly converted to offices, student hostels and bed and breakfast accommodation.

Bloomsbury is the home of the British Museum and the University of London. It is similarly the chosen site for a large number of hospitals, including the Hospital for Sick Children and the Homeopathic Hospital.

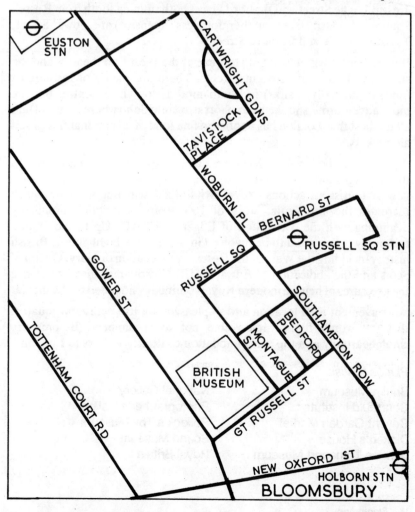

Last, but not least, it is one of London's foremost areas for holiday accommodation. The accommodation available consists not only of B&B's but also of a large range of two to four star hotels, the most outstanding of which is the highly ornate orange brick and terracotta "Hotel Russell" on Russell Square, opened on Derby Day, 1900.

It was some twenty to thirty years after this date that Bloomsbury became the home of a group of artists and writers known as "The Bloomsbury Set". These included the novelists E.M. Forster and Virginia Woolf, the art critic Roger Fry and the historian Lytton Strachey.

For those seeking B&B accommodation in Bloomsbury, the best street to try is Cartwright Gardens. Just five minutes from the hustle and bustle of Euston and King's Cross Stations, this is a quiet crescent of 18th century houses overlooking private gardens, the tennis courts of which are available for use by all guests. Two other very elegant streets of B&B's are Montague Street and Bedford Place, both running south from Russell Square. Less attractive (and therefore less expensive) are Gower Street, Tavistock Place and Bernard Street.

Bloomsbury is within walking distance of the West End theatres and the shops of Oxford and Regent Streets. There are plenty of restaurants (and, incidentally, banks) in Southampton Row in its centre, but the more adventurous should take a short stroll into Soho where they will find all the best that London has to offer in fine food of all nationalities to suit all pockets.

If you take a short walk to Euston Square, only three stops eastwards on the underground is the Barbican where you will find one of London's newest tourist attractions, Royal Britain, a fascinating museum which recreates the spectacular story of 1000 years of Britain's monarchy beginning with the coronation of Edgar in 973 AD. Up to the minute technology allows you to be involved in some of the highlights of British history including the Wars of the Roses, the execution of Mary, Queen of Scots and the abdication of Edward VIII. Visitors may also experience the pressures of being a modern Royal continually hounded by the media.

So convenient is its location and so pleasant are its streets and squares, that we would find it impossible not to recommend Bloomsbury wholeheartedly as a top accommodation centre for visitors to London.

Places to Visit

British Museum	National Gallery
Courtauld Institute	Photographer's Gallery
Covent Garden Market	Pollock's Toy Museum
Dicken's House	Soane Museum
London Transport Museum	Royal Britain

Albany Hotel

34 Tavistock Place
Russell Square
London
WC1H 9RE   Tel 071-837 9139

Price Band	££
Credit Cards	Access, Amex, Diners, Visa
Bathrooms	Shared
Television	In rooms
Breakfast	Continental
Telephone	Public
Parking	Difficult

In a street of indifferent B&B's, the Albany stands out. It has green and white canopies over the windows, masses of flower boxes, marble steps and even the tips of the black railings around the area are painted in gold! Inside it is plainer, yet there are little pot-plants in the bathrooms and prints on the walls. Bedrooms are on the small side, but they do have colour television and in-house video and tea-making facilities. It has a "family" feel to it – guests take breakfast around one large circular table and (most unusual for London) an evening meal is available on request, price around £7.00.

On my visit in 1989 I was pleased to find that the dining room had been embellished with a display of horse brasses, a cabinet of crystal glasses and that a feature had been made of the old kitchen range by adorning it with a copper kettle, an old flat iron and a whole series of little knick-knacks from days gone by. The manager has also opened up for guests' use a little patio full of flowers and trailing plants at the back of the house where afternoon tea is served.

Prices are a little on the high side, especially since the breakfast is Continental rather than English.

Travel Instructions: *Underground to **Russell Square**. Cross Bernard Street and walk along Marchmont Street until you come to Tavistock Place on your left. The Albany is on the left around the corner.*

Crescent Hotel

49-50 Cartwright Gardens
London
WC1H 9EL   Tel 071-387 1515

Price Band	££
Credit Cards	None
Bathrooms	Mostly shared, a few private
Television	In lounge
Breakfast	English
Telephone	Public
Parking	Difficult

The interior of the Crescent reveals an endearing hotch-potch of styles – the very English lounge is delightfully old-fashioned with thick, good quality carpet, solid black fireplace and highly ornate Regency mirror. The bathrooms are ultra-modern with Italian tiles, masses of natural light and numerous plants, giving them an air more of the Mediterranean than of England. Attractive pieces of furniture are dotted around the landings – a 1950's wickerwork chair in one corner and a handsome commode supporting a cheeseplant in another. There is a drinks vending machine in the hall.

The bedrooms are plain and comfortable and a few of the larger rooms have private showers.

The manager obviously takes a great pride and interest in her work. She even offers to loan rackets to those guests who wish to play tennis in the private gardens opposite. This Bed and Breakfast is suitable for all types of budget traveller.

Travel Instructions: *Underground to **Euston**. Turn left onto the main Euston Road. Walk along until you come to Mabledon Place on the right. This leads directly into Cartwright Gardens. The Crescent is on the right.*

Garth Hotel

69 Gower Street
London
WC1   Tel 071-636 5761

Price Band	£
Credit Cards	None
Bathrooms	Shared
Television	In lounge
Breakfast	English
Telephone	Public
Parking	Difficult

The Garth is a typical Gower Street B&B – cheap, plain, family-run and friendly. Good for people on a budget, especially students.

Travel Instructions: *Underground to* **Goodge Street.** *Cross Tottenham Court Road and walk along Chenies Street. Turn left into Gower Street and you will see the Garth on the left.*

George Hotel & Euro Hotel

58 Cartwright Gardens
London
WC1H 9EL   Tel 071-387 6789
                              071-387 1528
                      Fax 071-383 5044

Price Band	££
Credit Cards	Access, Visa
Bathrooms	Mostly shared
Television	In rooms
Breakfast	English
Telephone	Public card phone
Parking	Difficult

The George Hotel and the Euro Hotel are situated a couple of doors away from each other on Cartwright Gardens. They are run by the same manager and use the same telephone number for reservations. At the moment, although changes are in the pipeline, they are quite different in style. The Euro Hotel is very modern with decor in pastels, fashionable prints on the wall and a brasserie-style dining room and reception. The George, on the other hand, is far more traditional: patterned carpets and a functional dining room with lace curtains and a spray of flowers on each table. Rooms in both B&B's have a radio alarm and tea and coffee making facilities. Very good family rooms at the Euro Hotel. Note that the latter has only showers, no bathtubs.

Travel Instructions: *Underground to Euston. Turning left into the main Euston Road, take the third street on the right. This is Mabledon Place and it leads directly into Cartwright Gardens, where you will find the George and the Euro Hotels on the right.*

Gower House Hotel ═══

57 Gower Street
London
WC1E 6HJ   Tel 071-636 4685

Price Band	£
Credit Cards	*Access, Visa*
Bathrooms	*Mostly shared, but family rooms have private facilities*
Television	*In lounge*
Breakfast	*English*
Telephone	*Public*
Parking	*Difficult*

Run by a Maltese gentleman, the Gower House Hotel is one of the better B&B's on Gower Street. Decor in the public areas is in an unusual two-tone blue, whilst in most of the bedrooms beige predominates.

The most striking feature of this B&B is the tremendous variety of original fireplaces, some of which are of orange and green marble inlaid on dark wood and others of which are tiled in all sorts of attractive designs. They are nearly all surmounted by imposing antique gilt mirrors, thus forming an eye-catching focal point for the otherwise plain bedrooms.

As in so many Bloomsbury B&B's, the dining room and lounge are situated in the basement and are functional rather than eye-catching.

Travel Instructions: *Underground to Goodge Street. Cross over Tottenham Court Road and walk along Chenies Street. Turn left into Gower Street and the Gower House Hotel is on the left.*

Haddon Hall Hotel ═══

39-40 Bedford Place
London
WC1B 5JT   Tel 071-636 0026
                 071-636 2474

Price Band	££
Credit Cards	*Access, Visa*
Bathrooms	*Private and shared*
Television	*In lounge*
Breakfast	*English*
Telephone	*Public*
Parking	*Difficult*

Run by a Spanish lady, Haddon Hall is a very typical Bloomsbury B&B, with large ground floor lounge in pinks and greys and some thirty bedrooms, mostly decorated in autumn colours. There is a very large Spanish-style breakfast room with wood and basketwork chairs and fresh white tablecloths in the basement.

Excellent location close to the British Museum and Oxford Street.

Travel Instructions: *Underground to Holborn. On leaving the station, cross over to the "K" Shoe Shop and walk along Southampton Row, past Sicilian Avenue. Cross Vernon Place and then turn left into Bloomsbury Place. Bedford Place is then the first turning on the right and you will immediately see the Haddon Hall Hotel on the left.*

Harlingford Hotel ═══

61-63 Cartwright Gardens
London
WC1H 9EL   Tel 071-387 1551

Price Band	££
Credit Cards	*Access and Visa*
Bathrooms	*Private and shared*

Television	*In rooms*
Breakfast	*English*
Telephone	*Public*
Parking	*Difficult*

The Harlingford is one of the most attractive of the Cartwright Gardens Bed and Breakfast addresses. A welcoming entrance hall with modern-style chandeliers and flower arrangements leads to a tiny reception from which a friendly Welsh manager, surrounded by books and left-luggage, rises to greet his guests. They are accompanied along freshly painted, beautifully carpeted corridors, lined with simple prints, to comfortable bedrooms which, whilst not striking, are light and pleasant: floral wallpaper, candlewick bedspreads and spotlessly clean, tiled bathrooms. All rooms are being equipped with tea/coffee making facilities.

The Harlingford offers everything one would ask of a "bed and breakfast" – superb location, maximum comfort, a warm welcome and value for money. It is strongly recommended.

Travel Instructions: *Underground to* **Euston.** *Turn left into the main Euston Road and then take the third turn on the right. This is Mabledon Place which leads directly onto Cartwright Gardens. The Harlingford is on the right.*

Hotel Cavendish ═══════

75 Gower Street
London
WC1 6HJ   Tel 071-636 9079

Price Band	£
Credit Cards	*None*
Bathrooms	*Shared*
Television	*In lounge*
Breakfast	*English*
Telephone	*Public*
Parking	*Difficult*

This is a typical Gower Street B&B – simple, inexpensive and friendly. It has not one, but two breakfast rooms, both of which, though in the basement, are bright and welcoming.

Travel Instructions: *Underground to* **Goodge Street.** *Cross over Tottenham Court Road and walk along Chenies Street. Turn left into Gower Street and the Cavendish is on the left.*

Jenkins Hotel ═══════════

45 Cartwright Gardens
London
WC1H 9EH   Tel 071-387 2067

Price Band	££
Credit Cards	*Access and Visa*
Bathrooms	*Private and shared*
Television	*In rooms*
Breakfast	*English*
Telephone	*In rooms*
Parking	*Difficult*

The Jenkins Hotel is certainly one of the best of the Cartwright Gardens "bed and breakfasts". It really does have the atmosphere of a *home*, an attribute so lacking in many London B&B's. The large country-style kitchen with its scrubbed wooden table, ironing board casually propped up against the wall and television muttering quietly away to itself, serves as the reception office. An unconventionally dressed receptionist is a thousand times more helpful than her be-uniformed counterpart in a chain hotel.

Graceful flower arrangements abound in the public areas. Easy chairs and miniature bookshelves are tucked into little nooks on the landing. Everywhere the paint is sparkling and the carpets soft and welcoming. In the bedrooms, old-fashioned tile fireplaces form the focal point and in the corner nestles that wonderful modern invention – the tea/coffee maker. Each bedroom also has a fridge.

The breakfast-room is an equal delight – white lace tablecloths and curtains on a background of English farmhouse blue.

This charming B&B is naturally very popular, especially since it charges no more than its neighbours. It is therefore advisable to make reservations well ahead of time.

Travel Instructions: *Underground to Euston. Turning left into the main Euston Road, take the third street on the right. This is Mabledon Place which leads directly into Cartwright Gardens.*

Jesmond Hotel

63 Gower Street
London
WC1 6HJ   Tel 071-636 3199

Price Band	£
Credit Cards	None
Bathrooms	Shared
Television	In lounge
Breakfast	English
Telephone	Public
Parking	Difficult

The Jesmond has more the feeling of a home than most of the other B&B's in Gower Street. There is a large cabinet full of books in the basement and the owners obviously love to spend time just chatting with their guests. Bedrooms are plain and clean and have tea/coffee making facilities. Rooms on the back are especially favoured since they overlook the garden. There are several large bedrooms, making it particularly suitable for families, though of course all other types of budget traveller would be happy here too.

Travel Instructions: *Underground to Goodge Street. Cross over Tottenham Court Road and walk along Chenies Street. Turn left into Gower Street and the Jesmond is on the left.*

Mabledon Court Hotel

10-11 Mabledon Place
London
WC1H 9BA   Tel 071-388 3866

Price Band	£££
Credit Cards	Access, Visa
Bathrooms	Private
Television	In rooms
Breakfast	English
Telephone	In rooms
Parking	Difficult

The Mabledon Court Hotel is a special addition for 1990 – a completely new B&B in central London. Run with great enthusiasm by the son of Mr and Mrs Davies of the Harlingford Hotel (page 00), it is in some ways more like a hotel than a B&B. There is a lift (unusual in Bloomsbury B&B's) and there are hairdryers, tea and coffee-making facilities, shampoo, shower caps and other little luxuries in the bedrooms. Decor in the bedrooms and bathrooms is in beige and the bathrooms are all fully tiled. Please note that there are no bathtubs – showers only.

Downstairs there is a cosy lounge with comfy sofas and copies of *The Tatler*. Beside the lounge is a modern dining room with eye-catching limed oak chairs and vases of flowers dotted around here and there.

Strongly recommended.

Travel Instructions: *Underground to Kings Cross. Take the exit marked "Euston Road South". Walk along past the Wimpy Bar and you will soon come to Mabledon Place on the left. The Mabledon Court is 50 yards down on the right, just past the "Nalgo" building.*

Mentone Hotel

54-55 Cartwright Gardens
London
WC1H 9EL   Tel 071-387 3927
            071-388 4671

Price Band	££–£££
Credit Cards	None
Bathrooms	Private and shared
Television	In rooms
Breakfast	English
Telephone	Public
Parking	Difficult

Like most of the establishments in Cartwright Gardens, the Mentone is a very good family-run B&B. It is striking for its beautiful hanging baskets at the front and its pretty white courtyard at the back which is full of fuschias, hydrangeas and camelias.

The bedrooms and bathrooms vary in decor from one to the other and tend to be very large by London standards. Those at the front have lovely views over the little park and tennis court and some even have balconies.

Note that none of the singles has private facilities and that there are no bathtubs – only showers.

Travel Instructions: *Underground to **Russell Square**. (This is especially convenient if you are coming in from Heathrow Airport on the Piccadilly Line.) On leaving the station, cross Bernard Street and walk along Marchmont Street. At the end of Marchmont Street you will find Cartwright Gardens and the Mentone on the left.*

Morgan Hotel

24 Bloomsbury Street
London
WC1B 3QJ   Tel 071-636 3735

Price Band	££
Credit Cards	None
Bathrooms	Private
Television	In rooms
Breakfast	English
Telephone	Public
Parking	Difficult

The brother of the proprietor of the Morgan Hotel is a carpenter and it is thanks to him that this little B&B rates among London's top twenty. The entrance hall, which is at a slight angle, has been panelled in mahogany and mirrors have been set into each panel to create a feeling of space and opulence. The dining room is even more eye-catching. It is a light oak-panelled room with a fabulous display of china, arrangements of dried flowers and two cosy little niches at the far end. The bedrooms are furnished in maroon and grey and they all have elegant easy chairs. Note that the bathrooms have showers only; there are no bath-tubs. All windows have double glazing.

Prices, especially on singles, are very competitive, so the Morgan is naturally very popular. You are therefore advised to book at least two months in advance. Note also the superb location, just one minute from the British Museum.

Travel Instructions: *Underground to **Tottenham Court Road**. Walk along Great Russell Street past the Y Hotel and the YWCA. Turn left into Bloomsbury Street and you will find the Morgan Hotel on the right.*

Complaints

We very much hope that you will be happy with the B&B you choose from this guide. However, should you have any cause for complaint or suggestions for improvement, please do not hesitate to pass them on to the owner or manager, who will usually be only too keen to put things right.

If you have a serious complaint which cannot be settled on the spot, you should contact the London Tourist Board (071-730 3450) and you should also write to us. We will follow up all such complaints but we regret that we cannot act as intermediaries or on your behalf nor can we or the Publishers accept responsibility for any of the services or accommodation described.

The Ridgemount Private Hotel

65 Gower Street
London
WC1E 6HJ   Tel 071-636 1141

Price Band	£
Credit Cards	None
Bathrooms	Shared
Television	In lounge
Breakfast	English
Telephone	Public
Parking	Difficult

The Ridgemount is run by a very warm
Welsh family who make one feel
immediately at home. The large,
comfortable lounge has a "lived in"
look – a few pieces of redundant
furniture being stored at one end and
the armchairs being that tiny bit worn.
The bedrooms are all quite different
one from the other, some huge and
some tiny. Original marble and stone
fireplaces have been kept intact in the
lounge and in many of the bedrooms.

We would recommend the Ridgemount
to all visitors, but especially to families,
since the rates in a four-bedded room
are very reasonable and since children
would be assured of a warm welcome.

Travel Instructions: *Underground to **Goodge
Street**. Cross over Tottenham Court Road and
walk along Chenies Street. Turn left into Gower
Street and the Ridgemount is on the left.*

Ruskin Hotel

23-24 Montague Street
London
WC1B 5BN   Tel 071-636 7388

Price Band	££–£££
Credit Cards	Access, Amex, Diners, Visa
Bathrooms	Private and shared. Some private showers.
Television	In lounge
Breakfast	English
Telephone	Public
Parking	Difficult

The Ruskin Hotel is run by a friendly
Spanish family who take enormous
pride in their work and have obviously
spent large sums of money on
decoration and renovation. They have,
for example, laid attractive, pale yellow
terrazzo floors in the entrance lobby
and dining room; installed an ingenious
lift which opens on two sides, and
double-glazed many of the windows.
Since many rooms overlook the garden
at the back, they are ideal for visitors
seeking quiet accommodation.

There is an enormous (and yet cosy)
lounge with elegant curved door,
curved walls and corniced ceiling.
Décor in most parts of the building is
in pale yellows, mustards and browns.
A floor-to-ceiling mirror runs the full
length of one of the dining room walls,
giving an impression of even more
space!

There are hot and cold drinks machines
in a service area behind the lounge.
Note that there are no bathtubs, only
showers throughout. Everything is
spotlessly clean: a super B&B in a super
area.

Travel Instructions: *Underground to **Tottenham
Court Road**. Follow the signs for the British
Museum. Walk past the Museum and turn left into
Montague Street. The Ruskin is on the right.*

Russell House Hotel

11 Bernard Street
London
WC1N 1LN   Tel 071-837 7686

Price Band	££
Credit Cards	None
Bathrooms	Private
Television	In rooms
Breakfast	Continental
Telephone	Public
Parking	Difficult

The Russell House is a simple, value-
for-money B&B run by an Italian
gentleman. Bedrooms are plain with
attractively tiled bathrooms. *Note* that
there are no single rooms in this B&B.
The diningroom is exceptionally pretty.
A pale terrazzo floor sets off the dark
antique dresser and cabinet holding a
display of crystal. The tables are
covered with pale lemon cloths and set
with delicate white floral china. On the
window sills are two handsome pot
plants.

The Russell House is strongly
recommended, especially considering its
position right beside Russell Square
Tube Station.

Travel Instructions: *Underground to **Russell
Square**. You will find the Russell House on the
right as you leave the station.*

St. Margaret's Hotel

26 Bedford Place
London
WC1B 5JL   Tel 071-636 4277
              071-637 5908

Price Band	££
Credit Cards	None
Bathrooms	Shared
Television	In lounge and bedrooms
Breakfast	English
Telephone	Public and in bedrooms
Parking	Difficult

The St. Margaret's Hotel is a super
B&B in a super area. On the edge of
Russell Square, it is formed of a group
of four handsome Georgian houses and

has been managed by the same Italian family for the past forty years. There are two lounges, one "quiet lounge" with writing desk, sober coffee table and high armchairs and another, less formal with television, plastic-backed chairs and no frills. An excellent idea.

Between the lounges and the breakfast room is an exquisite panel of stained glass depicting a heron and a kingfisher on the edge of a lake. The breakfast room is spacious and bright; there is a little spray of flowers on each table.

Some of the bedrooms are quite ordinary, whilst others are most original. For example, one of the family rooms on the back of the house has its own tiled conservatory looking over the garden. There is originality also in the bathrooms – I was shown one which was decorated completely in green except for a thin frieze of pink, which reminded me of the bathrooms in my grandfather's house in days gone by. It is worth noting that the rooms on the back have a splendid view over the gardens – on my visit both the laburnum and the may were in full bloom, making a glorious backdrop to the bedroom.

Lastly, there is the warm Italian welcome which guests are sure to receive, making the St. Margaret's one of London's top B&B's in its category.

Travel Instructions: *Underground to Holborn. On leaving the station, walk along the left-hand side of Southampton Row. Cross Vernon Place and turn left into Bloomsbury Place. Bedford Place is the first right turn and the St. Margaret's Hotel is at the end on the left.*

Thanet Hotel ══════════

8 Bedford Place
London
WC1B 5JA   Tel 071-636 2869
                 071-580 3377
                 071-323 9053

Price Band	££
Credit Cards	Access, Visa
Bathrooms	Private and shared
Television	In rooms
Breakfast	English
Telephone	Public
Parking	Difficult

Glorious flower boxes draw one like a magnet to the Thanet. A riot of colour against deep Trafalgar-blue double doors and windows, all sparkling in the warm sunshine (on one of London's finer days, that is!) Inside the building everything is just as fresh, with thick carpets and shining paintwork. The dining room has a pretty maroon and cream carpet with matching tablecloths and a compact little breakfast bar at the rear.

The bedrooms are bright and the decor is mainly in pinks and pastel greens. As in so many of these old Bloomsbury houses, some beautiful tiled fireplaces are to be found in the bedrooms, all of which have radios and tea and coffee making facilities.

The breakfast menu changes according to the day of the week, which is a good idea since our English "fry-ups" can become somewhat monotonous after three or four days!

Prices are very competitive. One of Bloomsbury's best B&B's.

Travel Instructions: *Underground to Holborn. Cross at the traffic lights and walk along Southampton Row past Sicilian Avenue. Cross Vernon Place and turn left into Bloomsbury Place. Bedford Place is the first turning on the right and the Thanet is a little way along on the right.*

Wansbeck Hotel

4-6 Bedford Place
London
WC1B 5JD   Tel 071-636 6232
                071-242 2828

Price Band	££
Credit Cards	Access, Visa
Bathrooms	Shared
Television	In lounge and bedrooms
Breakfast	English
Telephone	Public
Parking	Difficult

The Wansbeck is a nice, friendly B&B in one of Bloomsbury's loveliest streets. The spacious lounge and diningroom are on the ground floor (as opposed to being in the basement as in most London B&B's) and are therefore extra bright and cheerful.

Generally speaking, the best rooms are to be found on the third floor (well worth the climb!) and since the rooms on the back overlook the garden, they are excellent for guests seeking a quiet night away from London traffic.

I was pleased to find that a new shower had been installed on the second floor and that a re-carpeting programme for the bedrooms, begun some time ago, was now complete. The bedrooms have in addition been equipped with tea and coffee making facilities.

This B&B is very popular with businessmen and tourists, many of whom return year after year.

Travel Instructions: *Underground to Holborn. Walk along the left-hand side of Southampton Row, cross Vernon Place and turn left into Bloomsbury Place. Bedford Place is the first right turn and you will find the Wansbeck on the right.*

Chelsea and Sloane Square

Chelsea, originally one of London's riverside villages, was for many years famous as an artists' colony, our equivalent of the Paris Left Bank. High rents and rates have now forced all except the most successful to seek cheaper if less romantically situated accommodation and the area has become colonised by the better-off from the world of pop-music, show-biz and fashion.

Lined with boutiques and restaurants of every description, the Kings Road is young and vibrant. Its name synonymous with that of Chelsea, this very long road runs the entire length of the area and it is here that is enacted, on Saturday afternoons, the parade of the "Punks" – those strangely dressed, orange and pink spiky-haired youngsters who seem to hibernate the rest of the week! The most attractive section is Cheyne Walk which has some fine examples of Georgian architecture and magical views, especially at night-time when the lights from the floodlit bridges twinkle seductively on the water.

Chelsea's most beautiful building is the Royal Hospital, designed by Sir Christopher Wren, and now home to the Chelsea Pensioners, the old soldiers who are a familiar sight in their scarlet be-medalled tunics. In the grounds here is held annually, in late May, that feast of colour, scent and floral achievement – the Chelsea Flower Show. A great event in the calendar of the garden-loving British, it has perhaps become a little too crowded in recent years for some tastes. The area immediately round Sloane Square is different from the rest of Chelsea, both in its architecture, stately tree-lined streets of tall red-brick houses, and its inhabitants: the "Sloanes" – high-born, elegantly dressed and often very rich. The square itself is a charming mixture of the two cultures with its flower stall and seats under shady plane trees. The Royal Court theatre, overlooking the square, shows mainly avant-garde plays. Restaurants abound in Kings Road and its environs and range from the cheap and cheerful to the supremely elegant.

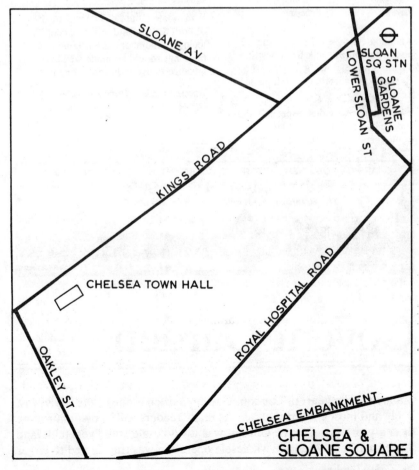

Transport: underground Sloane Square (Circle and District lines) and masses of bus services to all parts of London.

Places to Visit

Carlyle's House
Chelsea Physic Garden (summer)

National Army Museum
Royal Hospital

Annandale House ═══════

39 Sloane Gardens
London
SW1W 8EB   Tel 071-730 6291

Price Band	£££975
Credit Cards	None
Bathrooms	Private (except two rooms)
Television	In rooms
Breakfast	"London" (see below)
Telephone	In rooms
Parking	Difficult

Annandale House is ideally situated, just two minutes' walk from bustling Sloane Square, down a quiet road of elegant houses fronted by tall plane trees.

Everything is spacious, especially the bedrooms which are really large by London standards and contain tea/coffee makers and hairdryers. Furnishings have an old-fashioned charm and the overall atmosphere is one of great friendliness. Breakfasts are very much a feature here, different every day of the week. Eggs cooked in various ways, Welsh rarebit, kippers and, on Sundays, a special treat – hot croissants etc. served in the bedrooms. Kosher and vegetarian diets are willingly catered for. No bacon or sausages are served.

Annandale House has a loyal clientele of both tourists and business people, including members of Parliament, so bookings should be made well in advance to avoid disappointment.

Travel Instructions: Underground to **Sloane Square,** turn left and Annandale is just two minutes' walk down Sloane Gardens, on the left-hand side.

Covent Garden

Situated at the heart of London, Covent Garden is one of the city's most lively and most colourful areas. As many readers will know, until some fifteen years ago Covent Garden was a wholesale fruit, vegetable and flower market. When the wholesale operation was transferred to larger

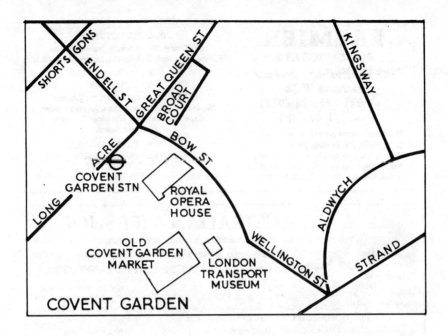

COVENT GARDEN

premises across the river, the market area (or Piazza, as it is called) was pedestrianised and numerous specialist shops, some restaurants and a pub were built into the original structure. In the market's central courtyard and in the cobbled streets on its perimeter is a delightful range of open stalls specialising in arts, crafts, hand-made clothes and antiques (the latter on Mondays only). Also on the cobbled streets and in front of St. Paul's Church are to be found London's best street entertainers – these range from jugglers and magicians to buskers and fire-eaters – fascinating to watch for adults and children alike.

Covent Garden is a very fashionable area with many designer dress shops, gift shops, collectors' shops, etc. and a huge selection of pubs, wine bars and restaurants lining the narrow 18th and 19th century streets. Last, but not least, it is the home of the Royal Opera House and some of the world's most famous theatres, including the magnificent Theatre Royal in Drury Lane.

Places to Visit

Bank of England Museum	Museum of the Moving Image
British Museum	National Gallery
Guinness World of Records	National Portrait Gallery
London Silver Vaults	Old Bailey
London Transport Museum	St. James's Park
	Sir John Soane's House

The Fielding Hotel

Broad Court
Bow Street
London
WC2B 5QZ   Tel 071-836 8305
                 Fax 071-497 0064

Price Band	££££
Credit Cards	All major
Bathrooms	Private, except for two singles
Television	In rooms
Breakfast	Continental (extra charge)
Telephone	In rooms
Parking	Difficult

Although not strictly a B&B, in the sense that there is an extra charge for breakfast, one could not possibly write a book on London's best small hotels without including the Fielding. Uniquely situated, within sight and sound of the Royal Opera House, down a small paved walkway lit by gas lamps, this eighteenth-century building has attractive diamond-paned windows and flower-filled window boxes. Push open the door into the cosy little reception, which doubles as a bar where, although the phone never stops ringing, the friendly manager always has time for a drink and a chat about the latest operas and plays. He will reserve your seats as well, plus booking sightseeing tours, etc.

The rooms, some in the form of suites with writing desks and armchairs, have theatrical prints adorning the walls and are full of old world charm. Bathrooms are modern and shining. The Fielding is, understandably, popular with many guests booking ahead from one visit to the next, so advance reservations are strongly advised.

Travel Instructions: *Underground to **Covent Garden**. Turn right and Bow Street is the third turning right, and Broad Court the first on the left.*

Earls Court

Earls Court is a cosmopolitan area on the west side of the city especially favoured by Australians. Close to the South Kensington Museums, it is famous for its two vast exhibition centres: Earls Court itself and Olympia, which play host to numerous world-famous events throughout the year, including Crufts Dog Show, The Ideal Home Exhibition and The Royal Tournament. It is a mixture of noisy streets (Earls Court Road and Warwick Road) and quiet, leafy squares (Nevern Square, Earls Court Square, Courtfield Gardens, etc).

The accommodation to be found in this area is also a mixed bag. A certain number of B&B's now house homeless families and should be avoided. On the other hand it is a *cheap* area with very good transport facilities, so by following this guide you will be able to find perfectly respectable, value-for-money accommodation.

Places to Visit

Brompton Cemetery
Commonwealth Institute
Geological Museum

Natural History Museum
Science Museum
Victoria & Albert Museum

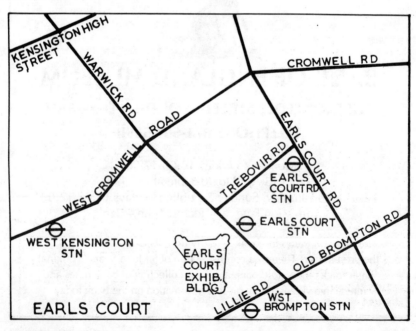

Amsterdam Hotel

7 Trebovir Road
London
SW5 9LS   Tel 071-370 2814
                  071-370 5084

Price Band	£££
Credit Cards	Amex
Bathrooms	Private
Television	In rooms
Breakfast	Continental; English extra
Telephone	In rooms, direct dial
Parking	Difficult

The Amsterdam is different from many London B&B's in that it has a very modern interior. There is a circular reception desk immediately inside the front door and a table with a delightful vase full of fresh flowers. Pastel shades predominate and furniture is a mixture of white painted wood and wickerwork. The tables in the diningroom are white, as is the crockery. On the walls are modern prints and everywhere there is masses of light. The presence of a lift makes it a good choice for anyone who dreads climbing the four or five flights of stairs which one normally finds in a more traditional B&B.

Travel Instructions: *Underground to Earls Court. Taking the Earls Court Road exit, turn left out of the station and first left again. The Amsterdam is on the right, just 1 minute's walk away.*

Centaur Hotel

21 Avonmore Road
London
W14 8RP   Tel 071-602 3857
                  071-603 5973

Price Band	££
Credit Cards	None
Bathrooms	Most rooms have en-suite bathrooms, remainder all have showers
Television	In rooms
Breakfast	English
Telephone	In rooms
Parking	On street (free)

The owner of the Centaur, a motherly lady from Yugoslavia, plainly enjoys every moment of running her B&B. She opens the door with a smile and likes nothing more than a chat over a cup of tea and a sandwich (available all day) in the cosy little breakfast room, where the walls are adorned with mementos from her country and gifts from grateful guests. Bedrooms are well decorated in pastel shades, and have nice wall lights and clock-radios.

Children are especially welcome, making this an ideal place for families as well as lone travellers, who may feel just a little bit lonely in the big city. Although it is only five minutes' walk from the Olympia Exhibition Halls, the Centaur is in a very quiet location.

Travel Instructions: *Underground to Olympia. Turn left and walk down beside the Exhibition Centre. Cross the Hammersmith Road and Avonmore Road is immediately opposite. Note: this station closes at 8 p.m. after which it is necessary to use West Kensington. Turn right, crossing West Cromwell Road, and the right-hand fork, Matheson Road, will take you to Avonmore Road.*

Concord Hotel

155-157 Cromwell Road
London
SW5 0TQ   Tel 071-370 4151/
                    4152

Price Band	*££–£££*
Credit Cards	*Amex, Visa*
Bathrooms	*Private and shared*
Television	*In lounge*
Breakfast	*English*
Telephone	*In rooms, direct dial*
Parking	*Difficult*

The entrance to the Concord is impressive, especially considering its modest charges. One sees past a central chandelier not only horizontally over a low reception desk to the garden, but also vertically to the top of an open stairwell where a clever plant twines its way heavenward in the fashion of Jack's beanstalk. Green carpets blend gently with green plants.

The family rooms are enormous by London standards and a number of them have private bathrooms and overlook the garden. (Note that the rooms on the front, however, overlook the busy main road to the west.) The lounge and breakfast room are equally spacious – traditional white linen tablecloths cover the tables. The staff are very courteous, making this one of Earls Court's better B&B's.

Travel Instructions: *Underground to Earls Court. Go out onto the Earls Court Road and cross over into Hogarth Road. This soon becomes Knaresborough Place. Walk to the end and turn right. The Concord is on the right.*

Henley House

30 Barkston Gardens
London
SW5 0EN   Tel 071-370 4111/
                    4112

Price Band	*££*
Credit Cards	*Access, Amex, Visa*
Bathrooms	*Private and shared*
Television	*In rooms*
Breakfast	*Continental*
Telephone	*In rooms, direct dial*
Parking	*Difficult*

Situated in what is probably the most pleasant road in Earls Court, looking over a shady garden square to the solid Victorian residences on the far side, Henley House is small sister to the Amsterdam (see above). Decor is a similar style: light and fresh-looking, mainly white with deep-pile green carpets, spotlights, and attractive touches – for example, the colours of the curtains are picked out in light switches. The fully tiled bathrooms are in restful shades of grey.

An attractive feature is the tiny first-floor seating area which has white wicker furniture, masses of plants and lots of glossy magazines to read! Henley House is certainly one of Earls Court's best B&B's.

Travel Instructions: *Underground to Earls Court. Take the exit to Earls Court Road which you cross, turn right and Barkston Gardens is the first left. You will find Henley House on the left.*

HENLEY HOUSE HOTEL

Overlooking a beautiful garden square in the Royal Borough of Kensington and Chelsea, the hotel offers 20 elegant and comfortable rooms, most with ensuite bathroom. All rooms have direct dial telephone and colour television. The courteous service and pleasant atmosphere have made us popular with tourists and business persona alike. Major credit cards accepted. Knightsbridge and the West End are within easy reach, as are the Earls Court and Olympia exhibition halls. The hotel is located off the M4 motorway and within 2 minutes of Earls Court Underground Station with its direct links with Heathrow Airport and Victoria Station.

30 BARKSTON GARDENS, EARLS COURT, LONDON SW5 0EN   TELEPHONE 071-370 4111

Mowbray Court Hotel ====

28-32 Penywern Road
Earls Court
London
SW5 9SU   Tel 071-370 3690
                 Fax 071-370 5693

Price Band	££-£££
Credit Cards	Access, Amex, Diners, Visa
Bathrooms	Private and shared
Television	In rooms
Breakfast	Continental
Telephone	In rooms
Parking	Difficult

The Mowbray Court is a sort of "queen" amongst London B&B's. Whilst the decor and general style are similar to an average B&B, the services which it offers are closer to what one expects of a far more expensive establishment. There is a lift, a bar, juke-boxes, TV monitors for security, a paging system, masses of tourist information, Fax and photocopying service available. The very enthusiastic staff are also happy to book tours, car hire and more or less anything else that is required of them!

On the whole, the bedrooms are larger than in many London B&B's and they all have radios. There are some very pretty bathrooms, carefully designed to fit sympathetically into the existing space.

The Mowbray Court has an annexe just two doors along and therefore has a large dining room with space for up to ninety guests.

An excellent B&B with an especial appeal to young people.

Travel Instructions: *Underground to Earls Court. Take the exit to the Earls Court Road, turn right as you leave the station. Penywern Road is the first turn on the right and the Mowbray Court is a hundred or so yards along on the right.*

Hotel Plaza Continental ====

9 Knaresborough Place
London
SW5 0TP   Tel 071-370 3246

Price Band	£££
Credit Cards	Access, Amex, Visa
Bathrooms	Nearly all private
Television	In rooms
Breakfast	Continental
Telephone	In rooms, direct dial
Parking	Difficult

The Plaza Continental was completely refurbished last year and although prices are on the high side everything is one hundred per cent fresh and sparkling. The reception desk is formed of a fine long block of mahogany and the manager standing behind it is very helpful and enthusiastic.

The bedrooms, which are plain and modern, offer tea-making facilities and hair-dryers. There is a lift to all floors.

Travel Instructions: *Underground to Earls Court. Cross the Earls Court Road, having taken the exit of the same name, and walk to the end of Hogarth Road where you will find Knaresborough Place and the Plaza Continental (5 minutes' walk from Underground).*

Terstan Hotel ====

29-31 Nevern Square
London
SW5 9PE   Tel 071-244 6466
                 071-835 1900

Price Band	££
Credit Cards	Access, Visa
Bathrooms	Most private; few shared
Television	In rooms
Breakfast	English
Telephone	In rooms
Parking	Difficult

The Terstan is located on a quiet, leafy square close to Earls Court Underground Station. Its bedrooms have a 1960's air about them – part panelled in wood-laminate and part papered in lime green woodchip wallpaper. Unusual for a London B&B, it has a bar (the receptionist will serve drinks to guests at most times of the day) and a pool table. There are also tea-making facilities in all the rooms. The Terstan is the ideal place for those who enjoy a chat and a drink with fellow guests at the end of a day's sightseeing.

Travel Instructions: *Underground to Earls Court. Take the Warwick Road exit and turn right out of the station. Then take the second right, which is the entrance to Nevern Square. Turn left and you will find the Terstan on your left.*

Kensington High Street

Kensington High Street and the surrounding areas offer everything the visitor to London could possibly want. Whilst the High Street itself is lined with an enormous variety of shops, from department stores to suppliers of artist's materials, the side streets are almost exclusively

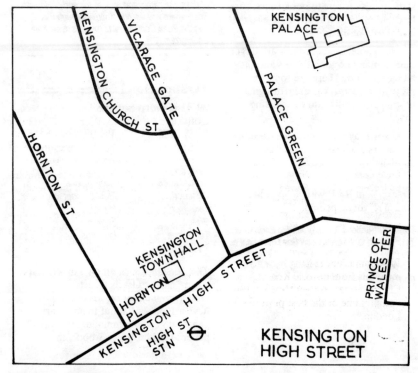

residential. There are many charming and peaceful squares within a stone's throw of the bustling shopping area. These are at their best in Springtime when the heavy clusters of pink flowers on the ornamental cherry trees transform the area into a veritable Wonderland!

To the north of the High Street are two streets of note: Kensington Church Street and Kensington Palace Gardens. The former is famed for its antique shops and the latter is nicknamed "Millionaire's Row" since it consists of a number of London's largest and most exclusive residences, many of which are now occupied by the embassies of various overseas countries.

Immediately to the east lies Kensington Palace (the London home of certain members of the Royal Family, including Prince Charles and Princess Diana) and Kensington Gardens, remembered fondly by many as the place in which spruce, uniformed nannies would walk the young offspring of the rich and famous in days gone by.

Transport is very good: Kensington High Street is on both District and Circle Lines and there are many bus routes. For restaurants, take a pleasant stroll northwards to Notting Hill.

Places to Visit

Commonwealth Institute	Natural History Museum
Holland Park	Science Museum
Leighton House	Victoria & Albert Museum
Kensington Palace	

Abbey House ══════════

11 Vicarage Gate
London
W8 4AG   Tel 071-727 2594

Price Band	££
Credit Cards	None
Bathrooms	Shared
Television	In rooms
Breakfast	English
Telephone	Public
Parking	Difficult

In an immaculate, leafy little road just moments from historic Kensington Church Street, Abbey House surely occupies one of the best positions in London.

One immediately notices the shining white paintwork and fine wide porch, flanked by marble columns. The floor of the hallway is in the original black and white terrazzo which is most attractive, amd from here an elegant staircase leads you to the comfortable bedrooms. Abbey House is run with the friendly professionalism which is such a joy to encounter and it is not surprising to find it is extremely popular, so bookings should be made well ahead to avoid disappointment.

Travel Instructions: *See Vicarage Private Hotel.*

Clearlake Hotel ══════

19 Prince of Wales Terrace
London
W8 5PQ   Tel 071-937 3274

Price Band	£££
Credit Cards	Access, Amex, Diners, Visa
Bathrooms	Private
Television	In rooms
Breakfast	Extra
Telephone	In rooms
Parking	Difficult

Although not strictly a B&B, in the sense that breakfast is not included in the room rate, Clearlake is too attractive in other ways to exclude from this book. The location is good, tucked behind some of Kensington's best hotels but with pretty views of Kensington Gardens from most of its windows. Accommodation varies from small singles to large apartments sleeping five or six. All are tastefully decorated and equipped with immaculate cooking facilities – just kettles and toasters in the singles to full kitchens in the apartments. For this reason most people prefer to make their own breakfast, although it is available in your room if ordered the previous night.

Other amenities include a lift, an attractive bar decorated with theatre posters, and, most important for back sufferers, excellent orthopaedic beds.

Children are made very welcome at the Clearlake and there are cots, high chairs and strollers for guests to borrow.

Travel Instructions: *Underground to High Street Kensington. Turn right and Prince of Wales Terrace is the fourth on the right. Note one of these turnings is a pedestrianised walkway only.*

Observatory House ══════

Hornton Street
London
W8 7NS   Tel 071-937 1577

Price Band	££££
Credit Cards	All major
Bathrooms	Private.
Television	In rooms
Breakfast	English
Telephone	In rooms
Parking	Difficult

This delightful B&B, situated in the most attractive part of Kensington, stands on the corner of Observatory Gardens – so-called because, for a time, it housed the largest telescope in the world. It is one of a row of town houses which are pure Victorian, and has been immaculately refurbished, keeping all its original character. Decor throughout is in shades of pinks and blues and the spacious rooms are really comfortable, with top quality beds, hairdryers and trouser-presses. One family suite is especially attractive, incorporating a small conservatory with lovely views over the surrounding gardens. Bath/shower rooms are in gleaming pink marble and most inviting.

The breakfast room, in Laura Ashley style, where the friendly Spanish staff will provide pots of tea or coffee at any time, is known as the Coffee Lounge and has low as well as high tables and armchairs – a relaxing and original idea.

Travel Instructions: *Underground to High Street Kensington. Hornton Street is directly opposite. Walk up the hill, about five minutes, and the house is on the left on the corner of Observatory Gardens.*

Vicarage Private Hotel

10 Vicarage Gate
London
W8 4AG   Tel 071-229 4030

Price Band	£–££
Credit Cards	None
Bathrooms	Shared
Television	Lounge
Breakfast	English
Telephone	Public
Parking	Difficult

The Vicarage just has to be the ideal B&B, and fits its name perfectly. Much which one would associate with a country vicarage is to be found here. In spite of its central location peace reigns and the only sound is one of birdsong from the surrounding trees and gardens. An elegant, curving staircase with wrought iron bannisters leads upstairs from the pleasant hallway passing, on the first landing, a wide, sunny window sill which houses a happy array of plants. On the day we visited a kitten was sleeping contentedly amongst them.

Bedrooms have even more of the country vicarage feel, unusually spacious with solid, old-fasioned furniture and flower-sprigged design wallpapers and bedcovers.

The Vicarage has been owned by the same family for the last forty years. They no longer manage it themselves but leave that to the friendly casually-dressed young manager who takes an obvious pleasure in being helpful. As this gem charges no more than many B&B's with half its charm and atmosphere it is, not surprisingly, booked up weeks even months ahead, so reservations must be made well in advance, especially for Christmas and the popular Summer months.

Travel Instructions: *Underground to **High Street Kensington**. Turn right along the busy High Street which you cross, turning left by St. Mary Abbotts Church, and walk up (literally uphill) Church Street. After two or three minutes walking the road forks – keep to the right and Vicarage Gate is the second on the right.*

Knightsbridge and South Kensington

Knightsbridge and South Kensington, linked by the broad thoroughfare Brompton Road, are after Mayfair, London's smartest areas. Still mainly residential, in spite of enormously high rates, every scrap of space is used to best advantage. The buildings, whether they be homes or offices, tall and palatial or tiny mews cottages, are uniformly well-kept which, combined with an almost total lack of litter in the streets, makes simply strolling around a great pleasure.

Knightsbridge is synonymous with Harrods, one of the world's largest and most famous department stores. In this vast terracotta building it is possible to buy just about anything on earth and to spend an entire day without seeing it all!

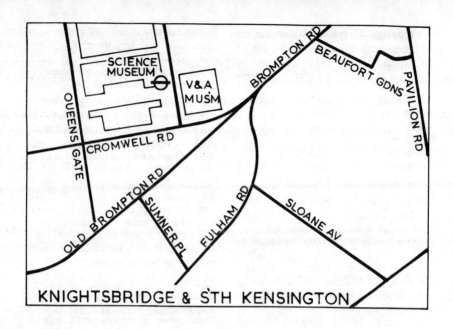

KNIGHTSBRIDGE & STH KENSINGTON

Also vast is the complex of museums further along Brompton Road at South Kensington. The Victoria and Albert (Museum of the Living Arts) Natural History, Geological and Science Museums are all here, each meriting many hours of the visitor's time. To avoid mental indigestion you may prefer to limit yourself to one or, perhaps two per visit to London!

A short walk from the museums brings one to the Royal Albert Hall, a huge amphitheatre, built in the mid-nineteenth century, where all manner of public gatherings and concerts are held. The best-known concerts are the Promenade Concerts, founded by Sir Henry Wood, which take place annually from mid-July to mid-September and are so-called because of the "Promenaders" – mainly young people who, for a fraction of the price of an ordinary concert ticket, can stand and listen to their favourite classical music.

Many architectural styles are represented in this part of London, from the Victorian ostentation of the museums and the pure beauty of Brompton Oratory to the charm of the white stucco houses that surround the squares of South Kensington, and the tiny flower-decked mews cottages (formerly stables) behind them. Incidentally the building unanimously voted by Londoners as the capital's ugliest is also here – Knightsbridge Barracks which was erected in 1970, a low spot in our architectural heritage and definitely to be hurried past as quickly as possible!

Restaurants abound in this district although prices do tend to be on the high side and visitors may prefer to venture slightly west, towards Gloucester Road in search of affordable meals. One small luxury, however, can be indulged here, for there are no two better places in London to take afternoon tea, that most English of customs, than Harrods and the Hyde Park Hotel. The latter is particularly delightful in summer, when the French windows of the elegant drawing room are opened onto Hyde Park.

Transport is exceptionally good in this area: two underground stations, Knightsbridge (Piccadilly line) and South Kensington (Circle, District and Piccadilly lines) and numerous bus services which serve all parts of the capital.

Places to Visit

Brompton Oratory	Natural History Museum
Geological Museum	Royal Albert Hall
Harrods	Science Museum
Hyde Park	Victoria and Albert Museum

Hotel 167 ══════════

167 Old Brompton Road
London
SW5 0AN   Tel 071-373 0672

Price Band	££££
Credit Cards	Access, Visa
Bathrooms	Private
Television	In rooms
Breakfast	Continental
Telephone	In rooms
Parking	Difficult

Hotel 167 is one of London's most stylish B&B's. Interior designed in Scandinavian style, the hall and stairways in shades of grey form a perfect introduction to the bedrooms, all different, which are full of colour and light. Venetian blinds, instead of curtains, let in the sun's rays while retaining privacy. Attractive pieces of antique furniture blend perfectly with modern colour schemes and extra features such as double-glazing, king-size beds and dimmer light-switches add to the feeling of comfort.

The 167 is very well-located and the owner and staff are friendly yet professional, making this an especially good place for younger, more sophisticated visitors.

Travel Instructions: *Underground to **Gloucester Road**. Turn right, walk down the road of the same name until you reach Old Brompton Road. Right again and you will see the 167 in a corner position on the opposite side.*

Kensbridge Hotel

31 Elvaston Place
London
SW7 5NN   Tel 071-589 6265

Price Band	£–££
Credit Cards	None
Bathrooms	Shared and private
Television	In rooms
Breakfast	Continental
Telephone	Public
Parking	Difficult

The Kensbridge is situated just two minutes' walk from the South Kensington Museums. It is an excellent budget B&B run by a friendly Irish lady. There is a lift, tea-making facilities and a fridge in all rooms. Apart from that there are no frills, but prices make it very attractive.

Since this B&B accommodates students during term-time it is normally only open to tourists during the holidays – in summer usually from May to September.

Travel Instructions: *Underground to **Gloucester Road**. Turn left out of the station and cross Cromwell Road. Continue along the Gloucester Road until you come to Elvaston Place on your right. The Kensbridge is on the right towards the end (ten minutes' walk).*

The Knightsbridge

10 Beaufort Gardens
London
SW3 1PT   Tel 071-589 9271
                 071-823 9692

Price Band	£££–££££
Credit Cards	Access, Amex, Visa
Bathrooms	Mainly private
Television	In rooms
Breakfast	Continental
Telephone	In rooms
Parking	Difficult

The Knightsbridge is a delightful little hotel, superbly situated in a quiet, tree-lined cul-de-sac, just moments from Harrods. Pinks and greys predominate in the restful decor; grey walls have pink bordering, carpets are soft and bedrooms stylish, fitted with tea/coffee making facilities and nice touches such as personalised matches, although it should be noted that some of the very large, and most luxurious rooms are on the expensive side.

Smart bathrooms echo the same colour-scheme and are well fitted with hair-dryers and masses of fluffy towels.

Highly recommended for discerning visitors looking for comfort and charm in a central location.

Travel Instructions: *Underground to Knightsbridge; turn left out of station, turn left along Brompton Road and, after passing Harrods, Beaufort Gardens is the third street on the left.*

Searcy's Roof Garden

30 Pavilion Road
London
SW1X 0HJ   Tel 071-584 4921
                  Fax 071-823 8694

Price Band	£££
Credit Cards	None
Bathrooms	Private
Television	In some rooms
Breakfast	Continental – served in rooms – £3
Telephone	Payphone
Parking	National Car Park – next door

Searcy's Roof Garden, as its name implies, is a most unusual B&B. Situated above an elegant suite of rooms (complete with butler!) which are used for wedding receptions and other functions, there is a separate entrance and lift which takes you to the roof garden. This is an attractive spot with wrought-iron seats and potted greenery. The fourteen rooms each have name and individual style of decor to match. There is one suite (suitable for a family), one double with a canopied bed, the rest being twins and singles. All, however, are charming with delightful touches – beds stand in wallpapered recesses and baths are in Victorian style. Considering the elegance of the location, prices are very reasonable – about half those charged by local hotels, which makes Searcy's a wonderful "find" for the discerning visitor. Please note, however, that neither VAT nor service charges are included in the quoted prices.

Travel Instructions: *Underground to Knightsbridge. Turn right and walk through Brompton Arcade on your right and turning slightly right at the end you will see Pavilion Road opposite the Basil Street Hotel. Searcy's is just two minutes' walk on the right-hand side. Each room has its own bell, so press the one marked "Manager" on arrival.*

Swiss House Hotel ══════

171 Old Brompton Road
London
SW5 0AN   Tel 071-373 2769

Price Band	£–££
Credit Cards	Access, Amex, Visa
Bathrooms	Private and shared
Television	In rooms
Breakfast	Continental
Telephone	In rooms, direct dial
Parking	Difficult

Pretty flower-boxes with ivy trailing over white balconies welcome guests to the Swiss House. Inside, the impression of a country B&B continues – russet carpets with soft apricot-coloured walls in the reception and dining area; soft pink walls and grey carpets in the bedrooms. Windows are double-glazed since traffic on the Old Brompton Road is quite heavy. Breakfast is self-service: the fruit, cheeses, croissants, *real* coffee etc. arranged on a Welsh dresser beside bunches of dried flowers in an earthenware pot. There is a large selection of room service snacks ranging from a simple sandwich to lasagne and chicken curry, available from noon to 9.00 p.m.

The manager obviously enjoys her work and takes every care to ensure that guests are really made to feel at home. The Swiss House is an exceptionally good Bed and Breakfast, certainly among London's top ten and is naturally very popular. Advance reservations are therefore imperative.

Travel Instructions: *Underground to **Gloucester Road**. Walk straight down the Gloucester Road over Courtfield Road and Harrington Gardens until you come to the Old Brompton Road. Turn right and walk another few minutes until you see the Swiss House on your left (10 minutes' walk from the Underground).*

Prices

We have sought to avoid the complicated symbols used in most guide books, retaining only one (£) to indicate the rates you may expect to pay. These are indicated thus:

£	Up to £32 Double/Twin Room Up to £22 Single Room
££	£33–£45 Double/Twin Room £23–£30 Single Room
£££	£46–£55 Double/Twin Room £31–£40 Single Room
££££	£56–£70 Double/Twin Room £41–£55 Single Room

(*Note:* Double = 1 large bed, Twin = 2 single beds)

These prices can, naturally, only form a general guideline, since they are subject to seasonal variations. **Always confirm prices when making a booking, and check that they include breakfast, VAT (tax) and service charges.**

Marylebone and Marble Arch

Marylebone, the area lying due north of Oxford Street, is an extremely convenient location for both the business and holiday traveller. Theatreland is but a stone's throw away, while for those planning a shopping spree not only Oxford Street (London's main shopping thoroughfare) but also the elegant smaller shops of Bond Street and South Molton Street are within easy walking distance.

It is this convenience, rather than any special charm, which makes Marylebone such a good choice for the visitor. Vestiges remain of the village it once was – notably Marylebone Lane and the delightful St. Christopher's Place, a pedestrianised walkway of restaurants and small specialised boutiques. Running parallel, James Street has a string of little restaurants which spill their tables onto the pavement, in true continental style, whenever the sun makes an appearance!

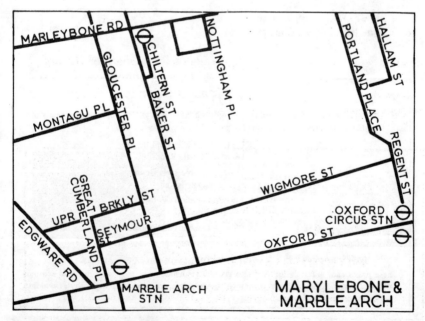

Marylebone is not, in the main, a residential area. Many of what were once homes are now offices and a large section is devoted to the medical profession – Harley Street being famous the world over for housing the consulting rooms of Britain's most eminent doctors.

Green spaces are somewhat few and far between. Sadly Montagu and Manchester Squares, though attractive, are private and therefore fenced off from the public. Tree lovers and joggers should fear not, however – Hyde Park is nearby, just beyond Marble Arch. Here you'll find the famous Speaker's Corner where anybody can stand up, usually on an orange box, and say anything they please, provided it is (just about!) within the law. This is quite an entertaining diversion on a Sunday morning and can be followed by a walk along Bayswater Road, where amateur artists display, and try to sell, their work. To the north of the area Regent's Park is also worth a visit, especially in June and July when Queen Mary's Rose Garden is quite a sight to behold.

Marylebone has plenty of restaurants in James Street and St. Christopher's Place (see above) while those looking for something a bit different should try the Swedish "Garbo's" in Crawford Street or the Afghan "Caravan Serai" in Paddington Street.

Transport, of course, is outstandingly good in this area. Four underground stations – Marble Arch, Bond Street, Oxford Circus and Baker Street and bus services too numerous to mention run services to all parts of the capital and beyond.

Places to Visit

Laserium	Regent's Park Open Air Theatre
Madame Tussaud's	(summer months)
Planetarium	Speaker's Corner
Regent's Park	Wallace Collection

Edward Lear Hotel

30 Seymour Street
London
W1H 5WD   Tel 071-402 5401

Price Band	£££–££££
Credit Cards	Visa
Bathrooms	Private and shared
Television	In rooms
Breakfast	English
Telephone	In rooms
Parking	Difficult

The Edward Lear is a fabulous B&B and wins top marks for both charm and friendliness. From the terrazzo-floored little entrance hall one has a choice of two lounges. One is quiet with a writing desk and armchairs; the other, complete with pretty Austrian blinds and deep sofas, contains the reception desk, an outsize TV set and masses of books for guests to borrow. The breakfast room, also on the ground floor, is furnished with Windsor chairs and has a polished wood floor for practicality. Menus on the tables exhort guests to "Eat, relax and enjoy".

Stairways, carpeted in warm russet, lead to comfortable, cosy bedrooms all fitted with tea/coffee makers and clock-radios.

Children are especially welcome at the Edward Lear. There are cots and high-chairs for guests to borrow and many young visitors have contributed to the "Artists' gallery" of drawings on the theme of Edward Lear, the famous writer of nonsense verse, who once lived in this house. Not surprisingly both this and its sister hotel, the Parkwood, are extremely popular so reservations should be made well in advance to avoid disappointment.

Travel Instructions: Underground to **Marble Arch**. Turn right and immediately right again into Great Cumberland Place. Seymour Street is the second cross street and you will see the Edward Lear almost straight in front of you.

Hallam Hotel

12 Hallam Street
London
W1N 5LJ   Tel 071-580 1166
          Fax 071-323 4527

Price Band	££££
Credit Cards	Access, Amex, Diners Visa
Bathrooms	Private
Television	In rooms and lounge
Breakfast	Continental
Telephone	In rooms
Parking	Difficult

The Hallam Hotel is superbly situated in a quiet street just moments from Oxford Circus. From the steps, one looks through the attractive glass and wrought-iron front door, flanked by lights, to the elegant interior. In the hallway and lounge enormous lamps stand on low tables and big leather armchairs look inviting, as does the small bar tucked in the corner. Bedrooms are restfully decorated in peachy colours, and especially popular are the three tiny singles known as "cabins" which are very reasonably priced considering the location. *Note:* no double or family rooms – only twins and singles.

The breakfast room, charmingly refurbished with wall-lights and pink table cloths, overlooks a tiny patio with plants – "a bit of green in the centre of London" as the manager says.

We highly recommend this lovely B&B to anyone who wants to stay right in the centre of London, yet in a quiet and friendly atmosphere. Like all the best places, it fills up very quickly, so bookings should be made well in advance.

Travel Instructions: *Underground to Oxford Circus, take the exit to the north side of Oxford Street, walk along Upper Regent Street, bearing left at All Souls' Church into Portland Place. A right-hand turn into New Cavendish Street brings you into Hallam Street, just opposite the Hallam Hotel.*

Hart House

51 Gloucester Place
London
W1H 3PE   Tel 071-935 2288

Price Band	££–£££
Credit Cards	Access, Visa
Bathrooms	Private and shared
Television	In rooms
Breakfast	English
Telephone	In rooms
Parking	Difficult

Hart House is typical of the upstairs/downstairs houses mentioned in the introduction. Ceilings are high with fine mouldings and both bedrooms and public areas are spacious. The combination of Welsh ownership and Spanish staff really works well here for everything is immaculate and one is quite dazzled by the shine on the paintwork and gleam on the windows.

A generous breakfast of four courses is served in the downstairs breakfast room.

Travel Instructions: *Underground to Marble Arch. Turn left again along Oxford Street and left again into Portman Street, which leads into Gloucester Place. Hart House is about five minutes' walk further, on the left-hand side. Many buses pass the door.*

Hotel Concorde

50 Great Cumberland Place
London
W1H 8DD   Tel 071-402 6169

Price Band	££££
Credit Cards	Access, Amex, Diners, Visa
Bathrooms	Private
Television	In rooms
Breakfast	Continental; English extra
Telephone	In rooms
Parking	Difficult

The first things one notices at the Concorde are the bright blue window blinds, and the little trees and carriage lamps that flank the front door.

Public areas are elegant. Delicately striped wallpaper forms a perfect background for Regency tables, one topped by an attractive dried flower arrangement in an antique china teapot. The lounge, where afternoon tea is served, and the small bar are equally lovely. Leather armchairs, large table-lamps, attractively lit paintings, and masses of antiques give the feeling of being in a private home. Bedrooms are comfortable but simpler with built-in furniture.

The Concorde is friendly and traditional. Bathrooms have tubs rather than showers and morning tea is brought to your room instead of making it yourself which is the norm nowadays. The presence of a lift is an added advantage, as is the fact that guests may use the restaurant and larger bar in the "big sister" hotel, Bryanston Court, next door.

Travel Instructions: *Underground to Marble Arch, turn right, and Great Cumberland Place is the first right.*

Hotel La Place

17 Nottingham Place
London

| W1M 3FB | Tel 071-486 2323 |
| | Fax 071-486 4335 |

Price Band	£££
Credit Cards	Access, Amex, Diners, Visa
Bathrooms	Private
Television	In rooms
Breakfast	English
Telephone	In rooms
Parking	NCP behind hotel

The Hotel La Place has recently been refurbished to a high standard and lifts have been installed. There is an elegant reception with an enormous bay window, an antique marble table and displays of silk flowers. The bedrooms are as luxurious as those of a three-star establishment. Colours vary from room to room – pinks, blues, green etc. – and furniture is a combination of mahogany and wickerwork. All bedrooms have tea-making facilities, trouser press, blow dryers and many even have a mini-bar.

There is an unusual dining room called "The Greenery Restaurant", and this is exactly what it is. Basket upon basket of artificial trailing plants hang from the ceiling, the walls are painted in pale green, and green serviettes stand out against white tablecloths.

Conveniently located for Madame Tussaud's and Oxford Street.

Travel Instructions: *Underground to Baker Street. Turn left onto the main Marylebone Road and Nottingham Place is the third turn on the right.*

Ivanhoe Suites

1b St. Christopher's Place
London

| W1M 5HB | Tel 071-935 1047 |

Price Band	££££
Credit Cards	Access, Amex, Diners, Visa
Bathrooms	Private
Television	In rooms
Breakfast	Continental
Telephone	Public
Parking	Difficult

The Ivanhoe Suites consist of six comfortable, well-furnished rooms above Plexi's restaurant, a candle-lit bistro which serves deliciously interesting food in extremely generous portions. Room rates are reasonable, considering the location – just one minute from Oxford Street yet quiet and traffic-free. St. Christopher's Place is a charming cobbled walkway, flower-filled in summer and magically decorated at Christmas-time, so perfect for shoppers at any time of year.

Travel Instructions: *Underground to **Bond Street**. Cross Oxford Street and Giles Court, which leads into St. Christopher's Place, is just in front of you.*

Kenwood House ═══════════

114 Gloucester Place
London
W1H 3DB   Tel 071-935 3473/
                  9455
                  Fax 071-224 0582

Price Band	££–£££
Credit Cards	None
Bathrooms	Private and shared
Television	In lounge and most rooms
Breakfast	English
Telephone	In hall
Parking	Difficult

Attractive striped awnings and well-filled flower boxes welcome you to Kenwood House. Inside, tranquillity is assured in spite of the heavy passing traffic, by efficient double-glazing. Bedrooms are well-proportioned and comfortable, all having good beds, hairdryers and pleasing colour schemes, while the Victorian feel to the public areas is enhanced by some large pieces of old mahogany furniture, including a piano.

The friendly owner, who formerly worked for British Airways (her husband still does), has tried to make Kenwood House the kind of place she would have liked to stay in on her former world travels. She has certainly succeeded. A warm, welcoming atmosphere prevails, staff are helpful and many little extras are offered, such as babysitting and trips to Heathrow or sightseeing in her own car.

Kenwood House is an outstanding B&B, especially in such a central location.

Travel Instructions: *Underground to **Baker Street**. Cross by the underpass on coming out of the station, turn right and Gloucester Place is the second on the left. Kenwood House is two or three minutes' walk down on the left. Many buses pass the door.*

Parkwood Hotel ═══════════

4 Stanhope Place
London
W2 2HB   Tel 071-262 9484

Price Band	£££–££££
Credit Cards	Visa
Bathrooms	Private and shared
Television	In rooms
Breakfast	English
Telephone	In rooms
Parking	Difficult

The Parkwood surely occupies one of the best situations in London: only five minutes' walk from Marble Arch, yet in a quiet street of elegant, porticoed

houses which opens onto all the splendour of Hyde Park. This is a gracious small hotel. Under the same ownership as the Edward Lear, it shares many of its attributes. There are comfortable bedrooms with tea/coffee makers, a spacious lounge/reception area, even the hand-written breakfast menus and "artists' gallery" of drawings by visiting children.

Travel Instructions: *Underground to **Marble Arch**. Turn right and after crossing the main Edgware Road, Stanhope Place is the first turning right. You will find the Parkwood on your left.*

Notting Hill and Holland Park

Travelling west from Bayswater one comes to Notting Hill, more residential and therefore more attractive than its neighbour. Some useful shops line the main road and a short walk to the north brings one to the famous and colourful Portobello Road Market (best on Saturdays) where anything over five years old tends to be sold as an "Antique". Bargains, however, are certainly to be found and even the non-collector can pick up an interesting oddment, which can make a far more appealing souvenir than the mass-produced articles sold in department stores.

South of the main road lies Hillgate Village, a pretty area of tiny, though very expensive town houses, each painted in a different bright colour, and beyond, as the road drops south towards Kensington (Notting Hill is literally on a hill) are some of London's finest residential streets (see Kensington section). Notting Hill is linked to Holland Park (called after the small park of the same name) by Holland Park Avenue, a broad thoroughfare lined with trees, behind which stand some good examples of Georgian architecture.

MAPS. The maps in *London's Best Bed & Breakfast Hotels* will give readers an indication of where places are – but since they are largely diagrammatic they cannot be precise or detailed.

We strongly recommend that readers use one of the easily available and inexpensive London Street Guides or Maps obtainable in bookstalls, kiosks and bookshops from such publishers as Geographer's A-Z, Yellow Pages, Geographia, Bartholomew's and Robert Nicholson. Maps are also available from the London Tourist Board and London Transport.

Eating places abound. If you are staying around here you could try a different cuisine every night without once stepping on a bus or underground! Hillgate Street has no less than three good Italian restaurants, Farmer Street is home to Geales – one of the best places in London to try our national dish, fish and chips – while the Ark, an aptly named little wooden building in Palace Gardens Terrace is so deservedly popular with locals that reservations are always essential. There are also several wine bars and the Greek and Indian places mentioned in the previous section are but a short stroll away.

Again, transport is excellent with two underground stations: Notting Hill (Central, Circle and District lines) and Holland Park (Central line) as well as many bus services.

Places to Visit

Holland Park

Kensington Palace

Leighton House

Portobello Road Market

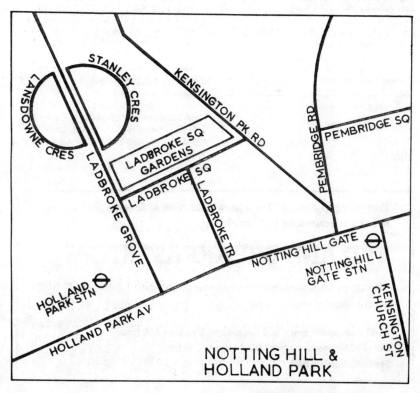

NOTTING HILL &
HOLLAND PARK

Mr & Mrs Demetriou Guest House

9 Strathmore Gardens
London
W8 4RZ   Tel 071-229 6709

Price Band	£
Credit Cards	None
Bathrooms	Shared
Television	In some rooms
Breakfast	English
Telephone	Public
Parking	Difficult

Demetriou's Guest House typifies the upstairs-downstairs houses mentioned in the introduction to this book. The bedrooms are spacious and many retain their fine moulded ceilings. Run by the same friendly couple for the last twenty years, it is spotless and welcoming with prices that are, especially for the area, incredibly reasonable.

Most rooms have three or more beds, so a good place for families (children are particularly welcome) or young people travelling on a budget.

Travel Instructions: *Underground to **Notting Hill**. Taking the exit on the south side of Notting Hill Gate cross Kensington Church Street, turn right into Palace Gardens Terrace and Strathmore Gardens is the third right.*

The Holland Park Hotel

6 Ladbroke Terrace
London
W11 3PG   Tel 071-727 5815

Price Band	££–£££
Credit Cards	All
Bathrooms	Private and shared
Television	In rooms
Breakfast	Continental, in rooms
Telephone	In rooms
Parking	Difficult

Good taste abounds in this charming B&B, situated in a tree-lined street just moments from the main road.

The building is a mixture of old and modern, but the two blend perfectly and little stairways and corners add to its interest. On the day we visited sunlight was streaming through the large windows on to the strategically placed pieces of antique furniture and Persian rugs. Each room has its own style and colour scheme with excellent beds, some brass, and tea and coffee making facilities.

During 1989 the two professional young managers have created a beautiful new lounge full of colour and light. As one of them says: "This is a fun place to stay" – and indeed it is definitely one of London's "top ten".

Travel Instructions: *Underground to **Notting Hill Gate**. Take the exit to the north side, turn left and after the row of shops Ladbroke Terrace is the first on the right.*

Paddington

Paddington is the area due north of Hyde Park. It takes its name from the main line station from where frequent, fast trains depart for interesting tourist spots like Oxford (59 mins) and Bath (1 hour, 20 mins) making it a good location for those who, while based in London, wish to explore other cities. Recommended for motorists in particular is Sussex Gardens, the only street in central London which has free off-street parking, and for families with children – many establishments here give discounts.

Hyde Park is a paradise for children. The large natural lake in its centre, known as the Serpentine, has boating and swimming in summer, two open-air cafes and a population of permanently hungry ducks and other water fowl who show off their fluffy offspring in April and May to the delight of residents and visitors alike. On one side of the Long Water which leads from the Serpentine to the Italian Garden at Lancaster Gate is a good play-park. On the other is a delightful statue of Peter Pan, immortalising in bronze the boy who never grew up. In Craven Hill is to be found by far the best children's museum in London – the Toy and Model Museum (admission charge) which contains a magical collection of childhood memorabilia and boasts a quaint toy railway in its garden.

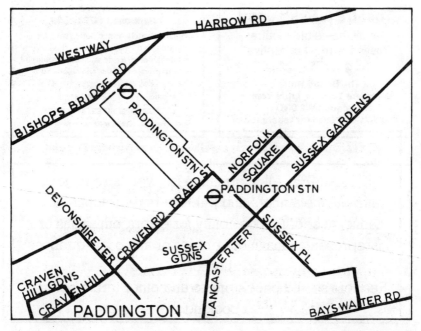

Restaurants in the area tend to be of the cheap and cheerful rather than the gourmet variety. Transport is excellent with many bus services as well as two underground stations; Paddington (Bakerloo, Circle, District and Metropolitan lines) and Lancaster Gate (Central line).

Places to Visit

Hyde Park

Little Venice

London Toy and Model Museum

Speakers Corner

Adare House

153 Sussex Gardens
London
W2 2RY   Tel 071-262 0633

Price Band	£–££
Credit Cards	None
Bathrooms	Shared
Television	In lounge and rooms
Breakfast	English
Telephone	Public
Parking	Limited parking on private road

Owned by the same family as the Moderna House further along the road, Adare House also welcomes visitors with a huge vase of lilies in the reception hall.

This is a good, plain B&B with a warm Irish welcome.

Travel Instructions: *Underground to **Paddington**. On leaving the station, walk along London Street past the Royal Norfolk Hotel. When you reach Sussex Gardens cross over and you will see Adare House behind the trees.*

Albro House

155 Sussex Gardens
London
W2 2RY   Tel 071-724 2931

Price Band	£
Credit Cards	None
Bathrooms	Shared
Television	In rooms
Breakfast	English
Telephone	Public
Parking	In front: 2 cars only

One of many good-value B&B's in this popular street, the Albro offers spotless, simple rooms at very competitive rates. Window boxes overflow with colour in true Italian style and owner, Mr Caruso, is friendly and welcoming.

Travel Instructions: *Underground to **Paddington**. Take the exit to Praed Street, turn right and first right down London Street which takes you into Sussex Gardens. The Albro is almost opposite.*

Allandale

3 Devonshire Terrace
London
W2 3DN   Tel 071-723 7807

Price Band	££
Credit Cards	Access, Diners, Visa
Bathrooms	Private
Television	In rooms
Breakfast	English
Telephone	Public
Parking	Difficult

In a street of indifferent B&B's, the Allandale stands out for its immaculate paintwork and bright, cheerful reception area where the moulded ceiling is prettily picked out in colour – Italian style.

Shower rooms are attractive, fully tiled in bright blue, but as these have been formed by taking a chunk out of the bedrooms it has left the latter very small. However, prices are among the lowest in London considering all rooms are en-suite with TV and English breakfast. Highly recommended for younger people who probably do not wish to spend too much time in their rooms.

Travel Instructions: *Underground to **Paddington**. Take the exit to Praed Street, turn left and Devonshire Terrace is the seventh turning on the right. This sounds much farther than it actually is, the area being densely populated.*

Balmoral Hotel

156 Sussex Gardens
London
W2 1UD   Tel 071-723 7445

Price Band	£
Credit Cards	None
Bathrooms	Mainly shared
Television	In rooms
Breakfast	English
Telephone	Public
Parking	Limited parking on private slip road

The wonderful thing about the Balmoral is that its bedrooms are larger than those of most London B&B's. There are welcoming flower boxes on the front windowsills and the receptionist is very friendly.

A good value-for-money B&B.

Travel Instructions: *Underground to* **Paddington.** *Walk along London Street past the Royal Norfolk Hotel and turn left into Sussex Gardens. You will find the Balmoral on the left.*

Camelot Hotel

45-47 Norfolk Square
London
W2 1RX   Tel 071-723 9118
                071-262 1980
                Fax 071-402 3412

Price Band	£££
Credit Cards	Access, Visa
Bathrooms	Mainly private
Television	In lounge and rooms
Breakfast	English
Telephone	Public
Parking	Difficult

Completely refurbished in 1989 under the artistic eye of the proprietor, Mrs Betteridge, the Camelot has now become one of Paddington's top B&B's. No expense has been spared to ensure that guests have every comfort – tea and coffee-making facilities, lift, luxury lounge-cum-reception etc. – in beautiful surroundings.

It is carpeted throughout in warm russet which pleasantly offsets light colour schemes and good lighting. A vast selection of antique and modern prints hang from the walls in the corridors and bedrooms. Unusually, one of the dining room walls is hung with the fascinating drawings of children who have stayed there and have been encouraged by the management to display their artistic talents. There are in fact two interconnecting dining rooms with exposed brick walls, red tablecloths and antique wooden dresser. The presence of a high chair is the second testimony to the warm reception that children may expect to find here. Highly recommended.

Travel Instructions: *Underground to* **Paddington.** *From the exit in Praed Street turn right, then first right into London Street and Norfolk Square is on your left. Camelot Hotel is at the far end, on the right.*

Dylan Hotel

14 Devonshire Terrace
London
W2 3DW   Tel 071-723 3280

Price Band	££
Credit Cards	None
Bathrooms	Private and shared
Television	Lounge
Breakfast	English
Telephone	Public
Parking	Difficult

This traditional style B&B has been owner-managed by Mr and Mrs Griffiths for many years. Bedrooms are of a good size and comfortable. About a third have en-suite facilities and all are equipped with tea/coffee makers, good beds and duvets.

Decor is old-fashioned, and we feel the Dylan will appeal most to middle-aged and older people who will appreciate the spaciousness of its rooms.

Travel Instructions: *Underground to **Paddington**. Take the exit to Praed Street, turn left and Devonshire Terrace is the seventh turning on the right. Not as far as it sounds!*

Europa House
151 Sussex Gardens
London
W2 2RY   Tel 071-723 7343

Price Band	££
Credit Cards	*Access, Amex, Visa*
Bathrooms	*Private*
Television	*In rooms*
Breakfast	*English*
Telephone	*Public*
Parking	*Limited parking on private slip-road*

The Europa House is a simple B&B run by a very friendly Spanish family. The dining room and bedrooms are plain and the bathrooms are tiled in fresh blues. Everything is spotlessly clean. Prices are amongst the lowest in London, so Europa House is ideal for visitors seeking real value-for-money.

On a recent visit I noted with pleasure new marble-effect wallpaper in hallways and the addition of attractive "Christopher Wray" lampshades. These improvements have been achieved without significant price rises, making this lovely little B&B even better value.

Travel Instructions: *Underground to **Paddington**. Walk along London Street past the Royal Norfolk Hotel and turn left into Sussex Gardens. You will see Europa House on the right behind the trees.*

Mitre House
180 Sussex Gardens
London
W2 1TU   Tel 071-262 0653

Price Band	£££
Credit Cards	*Access, Amex, Diners, Visa*
Bathrooms	*Private*
Television	*In rooms*
Breakfast	*English*
Telephone	*In rooms*
Parking	*Plenty*

Mitre House, while quite large for a B&B and containing many extra facilities such as a lift and a bar, has in abundance that essential friendliness which we looked for when researching this guide. Owner-managed by a delightful family, originally from Cyprus, who really care about their guests' welfare and hand-pick their staff to offer the same welcome.

Colour schemes throughout are in pinky-beiges, bedrooms are restful and bathrooms immaculate. Family suites are a feature: two rooms sharing a bathroom, totally self-contained and an excellent idea for parents who want to keep an eye on their youngsters while retaining some privacy!

Mitre House is a lovely place for all visitors, so it is fortunate they have added a number of new rooms during 1989.

Travel Instructions: *Underground to **Paddington**. From the exit in Praed Street turn left and take the first left, Spring Street, which takes you into Sussex Gardens and you will see Mitre House on the corner.*

Moderna House

18 Sussex Gardens
London
W2 1UL   Tel 071-723 2219

Price Band	£–££
Credit Cards	None
Bathrooms	Mostly shared, a few private
Television	In lounge and rooms
Breakfast	English
Telephone	Public
Parking	Limited parking on private road

Well-tended flower boxes on the window sills and a vase of lilies and carnations on a marble table in the entrance hall are a good indication that Moderna House is one of Paddington's better B&B's.

The bedrooms are simple and pleasant with some co-ordinated bedcovers and curtains and many new carpets. The dining room is traditional in style and has some very elegant padded chairs, the backs of which are inlaid with a design in marquetry.

It is run by a couple from Ireland, which country is renowned for its hospitality. A good B&B for all budget visitors.

Travel Instructions: *Underground to Edgware Road. Walk along the Edgware Road in the direction of Marble Arch. You will soon find Sussex Gardens on the right. Walk along another few hundred yards and you will see the Moderna on your right.*

Nayland Hotel

132 Sussex Gardens
London
W2 1UB   Tel 071-723 4615
                Fax 071-402 3292

Price Band	£££
Credit Cards	All major
Bathrooms	Private
Television	In rooms
Breakfast	English
Telephone	In rooms
Parking	Space for 2/3 cars

Re-opened in July 1989 after total refurbishment the Nayland is bright, fresh and welcoming. Well-fitted bedrooms, though not large, are comfortable and boast videos as well as TV and tea/coffee-making facilities. There is a small bar and the brand new, efficient lift is a blessing for those with luggage. The delightful manager, Tony, always remains calm and friendly no matter how much pressure there is from ringing phones and clamouring guests!

Travel Instructions: *Underground to Paddington, walk along London Street past the Royal Norfolk hotel and turn left into Sussex Gardens. You will find the Nayland on your left.*

Niki Hotel

16 London Street
London
W2 1HL   Tel 071-724 4466

Price Band	£££
Credit Cards	Access, Amex, Diners, Visa
Bathrooms	Private
Television	In rooms
Breakfast	Continental
Telephone	In rooms
Parking	Difficult

It is certainly a pleasant experience to step inside the light, cool interior of the Niki from busy London Street. Beyond the reception area, with its tiled floor and pastel walls adorned with modern prints, is a lounge/bar from where an attractive white spiral staircase, festooned with plants, leads to the roof terrace. More plants and seating are there for guests to enjoy the sun – when it appears!

The bedrooms, which are reached by either lift or staircase, are pleasant with pretty bedcovers matching the curtains and more prints on the plain walls. Bathrooms are especially good at the Niki: large and fully-tiled, the majority having both tubs and super-powerful showers, not, as one usually finds, simply hand-showers.

Breakfast is served in the Taverna Restaurant downstairs and offers, the manager assured me, "something different" every day. Discounts on other meals also available.

The Niki has recently undergone total refurbishment and is consequently in pristine condition, offering a high standard of accommodation with plenty of Greek style, in a central, if somewhat busy location.

Travel Instructions: *Underground to* **Paddington.** *Take the exit into Praed Street, turn right and London Street is the first on the right.*

Olympic House Hotel ═══

138 Sussex Gardens
London
W2 1UB   Tel 071-723 5935

Price Band	££
Credit Cards	*Access, Amex, Diners, Visa*
Bathrooms	*Nearly all private*
Television	*In rooms*
Breakfast	*English*
Telephone	*In rooms*
Parking	*Limited parking on private slip road*

Beautiful flower boxes welcome guests to Olympic House, which is run by a charming family from Cyprus. The reception area is spacious and includes a lounge section where cold drinks and free real coffee are available throughout the day.

The decor is in beiges and browns with mahogany fittings in bedrooms; bathrooms are tiled floor to ceiling.

A good budget B&B for all budget visitors.

Travel Instructions: *Underground to* **Paddington.** *Walk along London Street past the Royal Norfolk Hotel and turn left into Sussex Gardens. You will find the Olympic and Beverley House on the left.*

Picton House Hotel ═══

122 Sussex Gardens
London
W2 1UB   Tel 071-723 5479

Price Band	£–££
Credit Cards	*Access, Amex, Diners, Visa*
Bathrooms	*Private and shared*
Television	*In rooms*
Breakfast	*English*
Telephone	*Public*
Parking	*Difficult*

Picton House is a good, simple B&B run by a Spanish family who particularly welcome children. Outside, around the railings, are wonderful boxes of geraniums and trailing plants, the especial hallmark of a Spanish proprietor! Bedrooms are plain and comfortable and the dining room distinguishes itself with some unusual Scandinavian-style tubular steel chairs. On my visit a little boy was playing in the dining room, giving Picton House more of a "family at home" feel to it than most London B&B's.

Travel Instructions: *Underground to* **Paddington.** *Walk along London Street, past the Royal Norfolk Hotel and turn left into Sussex Gardens. Picton House is on the left.*

Queensway Hotel ═══

149 Sussex Gardens
London
W2 2RY   Tel 071-723 7749

Price Band	£££
Credit Cards	*Access, Diners, Visa*
Bathrooms	*Private*
Television	*In rooms*
Breakfast	*English*
Telephone	*In rooms*
Parking	*Limited parking on private slip road*

Queensway Hotel has just been completely refurbished to a very high standard and with a good deal of imagination. Decor in the reception area is in soft pinks and blues. An attractive mirror and wood coffee table reflects the cornices around the ceiling, whilst other wall mirrors reflect strategically placed plants and huge, glittering table lamps.

The dining room is similarly luxurious with lots of modern prints lining the walls. Bedrooms are amongst the most attractive of London B&B's (they all have tea-making facilities) and some of the bathrooms are even more spacious and light than those of a three-star hotel. Four of these now include Jacuzzi baths giving an extra touch of luxury to this delightful and ever-improving little hotel.

The Queensway Hotel is one of London's top twenty B&B's.

Travel Instructions: *Underground to* **Paddington.** *Walk along London Street past the Royal Norfolk Hotel. Turn left into Sussex Gardens and you will see Queensway House on the right behind the trees.*

Soho

Soho is the throbbing heart of London – colourful, crowded and cosmopolitan. It is the centre of lively Chinese and Italian communities and the best place in the whole of the city for eating out. It is also the main "red-light" district but tourists need not fear being pestered or even approached as they might in other capital cities. All in all, a fabulous place to visit yet, sadly, there is only one B&B in Soho: Manzi's.

Places to Visit

Berwick St. Market
British Museum
Covent Garden Market
Design Centre

Guinness World of Records
Hippodrome Nightclub
Museum of Mankind
Royal Academy of Arts

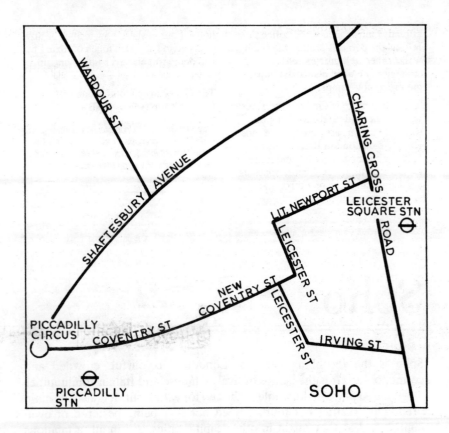

Manzi's

1-2 Leicester Street
London
WC2H 7BL   Tel 071-734 0224/
                0225

Price Band	£££
Credit Cards	Access, Amex, Diners, Visa
Bathrooms	Private
Television	In rooms
Breakfast	Continental
Telephone	In rooms
Parking	Very difficult

Manzi's is unusual for two reasons: firstly because of its unexpected location in the heart of Soho and secondly because it is in fact part of a famous Italian sea-food restaurant, consisting of a main ground-floor restaurant and a first-floor "cabin" in which guests take breakfast. This is a "fun" room, adorned with fishermen's nets, ships' lanterns, plastic lobsters and enticing mermaids . . .

Most of the bedrooms are on the large side (by London, not US standards!) and very comfortable. The two single rooms represent particularly good value at £35 apiece (1990). Note that there is a lift and that tea and coffee-making facilities are provided in the bedrooms.

A serious receptionist of the old school receives guests in the ground floor lobby, whilst she hands diners their coats and bids them goodbye. Manzi's is a true bastion of respectability in the maze of Soho's nightclubs and sex shops.

Travel Instructions: *Underground to **Piccadilly Circus**. Walk along Coventry Street and take the fourth left turn. This is Leicester Street and Manzi's is on the left.*

Victoria

Victoria seems to have become an area of budget accommodation mainly
due to the presence of its enormous station which handles visitors
travelling both via Gatwick and via the continental boat-trains. Most of
the so-called "Victoria" B&B's (note that they are of varying standards),
are actually situated either in Pimlico or in Ebury Street which is on the
very edge of Belgravia. Whilst Victoria has little to recommend it apart
from the neo-Byzantine Westminster Cathedral, squashed incongruously
between McDonalds and the 'K' Shoe Shop, Pimlico and Belgravia both
have very distinct characters.

PIMLICO is an area of big, white, terraced houses now converted to flats
and B&B's. There are strong Spanish and Italian contingents operating in
the area, evidence of which is to be found in the delicatessens,
restaurants, shops and market stalls around Tachbrook Street, Denbigh
Street and Warwick Way which form the district's focal point.

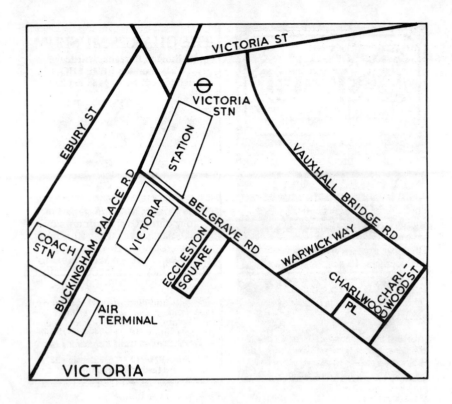

BELGRAVIA is one of London's richest residential quarters. Like Pimlico, it also consists of solid white Victorian terraces, though here they are even more imposing. Tucked away behind the terraces lie a series of charming cobbled mews, the balconies of which are brimming over with brightly coloured flowers and trailing plants.

Many countries have their embassies in Belgravia and there is usually a strong police presence accompanied by a glorious absence of litter!

Places to Visit

Buckingham Palace
Houses of Parliament
Guards Chapel
Guards Museum
Royal Mews

Queen's Gallery
Tate Gallery
St. James's Park
Westminster Abbey

Astors

110-112 Ebury Street
London
SW1W 9QU   Tel 071-730 3811

Price Band	£££
Credit Cards	Access, Visa
Bathrooms	Shared and private
Television	In rooms
Breakfast	English
Telephone	Public
Parking	Difficult

Astors is a very typical London B&B, close to Victoria Coach and Railway Stations. Bedrooms are plain but do all have tea and coffee making facilities. There is a pretty little dining room in the basement. Its walls are painted in pure white, tablecloths are blue and yellow, a pale blue blind diffuses a soft light and tied back curtains make a special feature of the windows.

Travel Instructions: *Underground or British Rail to Victoria. On leaving the station, walk along the Buckingham Palace Road past the Grosvenor Hotel and turn right into Eccleston Street. Then turn left into Ebury Street and you will soon see Astors on the right.*

Cartref House

129 Ebury Street
London
SW1W 9QU   Tel 071-730 6176

Price Band	££
Credit Cards	None
Bathrooms	Private and shared
Television	In rooms
Breakfast	English
Telephone	Payphone
Parking	Difficult

Cartref House is the kind of warmly-welcoming, very British B&B that is hard to find in central London. Bedrooms, all with tea/coffee makers, are in pleasantly cool colour schemes and everything absolutely shines. The cosy downstairs breakfast room has Windsor chairs and masses of ornaments and pictures and is a happy, friendly place to start the day. *Please note:* Cartref House is closed from just before Christmas until the end of March while the owners, who work hard all year ensuring their guests' comfort and often serve breakfast themselves, take a well-earned vacation.

Travel Instructions: *Underground to Victoria. From the station forecourt turn left into Buckingham Palace Road. After crossing the road, a right turn into Eccleston Street takes you into Ebury Street and you will see Cartref on your left.*

Chesham House Hotel

64 Ebury Street
London
SW1 W9Q   Tel 071-730 8513
                    Telex 946 797
                    Pronto-G att:
                    C.S.P.

Price Band	££
Credit Cards	*Access, Amex, Diners, Visa*
Bathrooms	*Shared*
Television	*In rooms*
Breakfast	*English*
Telephone	*Public (Cardphone)*
Parking	*Difficult*

The Chesham House is a good B&B with a handsome wooden and glass entrance door. Decor is generally beiges and browns; bedrooms plain and comfortable with the unusual addition of a trouser press. Bathrooms and showers are large by London standards and have recently been tiled and modernised. In the two-part breakfast room are "fun" green and orange wooden chairs and somebody has taken great care to cover crockery, etc. with tea-cloths, lest the tiniest speck of dust should fall on an unsuspecting cup or saucer! Complimentary real coffee, served in the lounge from 5pm, is a pleasing extra.

A thoroughly respectable and conveniently located B&B.

Travel Instructions: *Underground or train to Victoria. Make your way to the Grosvenor Hotel and walk up Lower Belgrave Street which lies opposite it. Turn left into Ebury Street and walk a few minutes more. You will find the Chesham House on your right.*

Collin House

104 Ebury Street
London
SW1W 9QD   Tel 071-730 8031

Price Band	££
Credit Cards	*None*
Bathrooms	*Private and shared*
Television	*None*
Breakfast	*English*
Telephone	*Payphone*
Parking	*Difficult*

Collin House fulfills every criteria of a good B&B. It is warm, welcoming and spotless and the Welsh owners and Spanish staff always make guests feel "at home". Bedrooms are of a good size and prettily furnished in Laura Ashley style, while the breakfast room is cosy and the breakfast generous. Prices are very fair and it is not surprising that Collin House is one of London's most popular B&B's. Advance reservations are therefore essential.

Travel Instructions: *Underground or train to Victoria, turn left out of the station forecourt into Buckingham Palace Road. Cross, and any right-hand turning takes you into Ebury Street. Collin House is on the right.*

Eaton House

125 Ebury Street
London
SW1 9QU   Tel 071-730 8781

Price Band	££
Credit Cards	*Access, Amex, Visa*
Bathrooms	*Shared*
Television	*In rooms*
Breakfast	*English*
Telephone	*Public*
Parking	*Difficult*

Eaton House is a very typical London B&B, run by the same Spanish family for the last 23 years. We were pleased on our visit this year to find that attractive deep blue and grey flecked carpets have been installed in the public areas and to hear that shortly the rest of the house will be freshly carpeted and the breakfast room re-fitted.

Although this is a fairly plain B&B, the charming owner does much to make it feel special and we envisage that it will go from strength to strength.

Travel Instructions: *Underground or train to* **Victoria,** *turn left out of the station forecourt into Buckingham Palace Road. Cross, and any right-hand turning takes you into Ebury Street. Eaton House is on the left-hand side.*

Ebury House ═══════════

102 Ebury Street
London
SW1 9QD   Tel 071-730 1350/
                 1059

Price Band	££
Credit Cards	None
Bathrooms	Shared
Television	In rooms
Breakfast	English
Telephone	Public
Parking	Difficult

Ebury House is one of the best B&B's in Ebury Street. Bedrooms have that little bit of extra comfort – ruched curtains, hair-dryers, etc. – and greater than normal attention is paid to cleanliness and general standards. Rooms on the front have double-glazing.

I was shown around by a friendly Spanish lady who, although not actually the owner, takes a tremendous pride in her work. Prices are a couple of pounds higher than those along the street, but well worth the extra.

Travel Instructions: *Underground or BR to* **Victoria.** *Walk along Buckingham Palace Road in the direction of the Coach Station and turn right into Eccleston Street. Then turn left into Ebury Street and you will find Ebury House on the right.*

Elizabeth Hotel ═══════════

37 Eccleston Square
London
SW1V 1PB   Tel 071-828 6812/
                 6813

Price Band	££–£££
Credit Cards	None
Bathrooms	Private and shared
Television	Lounge and in en-suite rooms
Breakfast	English (Continental for early departures)
Telephone	Payphone
Parking	Difficult

The Elizabeth is one of Victoria's best and most popular B&B's, mentioned in countless guide books and having won an award from the British Tourist Authority as one of London's top B&B's in its class. It certainly stands out from its neighbours with its pretty yellow paintwork and its favourable position, facing directly onto leafy Eccleston Square, where guests may relax or play tennis if they wish.

Public rooms are most pleasing, spacious and furnished in the slightly old-fashioned style which gives a feeling of permanence. Some double and family rooms are very comfortable with TV, fridges and armchairs, as well as private bathrooms, while singles are small and simple. All, however, are quiet and spotless.

The Elizabeth has a loyal and devoted clientele, so potential guests should write well in advance to avoid disappointment.

Travel Instructions: *Train, underground or bus to* **Victoria.** *From the station forecourt turn left along Buckingham Palace Road; take the second left, Elizabeth Bridge, leading into St. George's Drive and you will come very soon to the Elizabeth on your right. From Victoria Coach Station it is even nearer: just walk straight ahead, over Elizabeth Bridge.*

Enrico Hotel

79 Warwick Way
London
SW1V 1QP   Tel 071-834 9538

Price Band	£
Credit Cards	None
Bathrooms	Shared; some private showers
Television	In lounge
Breakfast	English
Telephone	Public
Parking	Difficult

The facade of the Enrico Hotel stands out from the others in the street. It is sparkling white with window ledges and surrounds picked out in orange, as are the tips of the white railings.

Inside, everything is just as fresh and sparklingly clean. Bedrooms are pretty with little alcoves and delicate prints of flowers etc., but the dining room is its *piece de resistance*. It is decorated in soft blues with a tiny touch of green in the carpet. The curtains are obviously of very good quality and worthy of a far more expensive establishment. There is a gently curved archway between its two sections, pretty lamps on the wall, dado rail breaking the lines of the wallpaper, etc.

An excellent value-for-money B&B.

Travel Instructions: *Underground or BR to* **Victoria.** *Walk along Buckingham Palace Road past the Grosvenor Hotel and turn left into Eccleston Bridge which runs into Belgrave Road. Walk a few minutes along here and turn right into Warwick Way. Enrico Hotel is on the right.*

Hamilton House

60 Warwick Way
London
SW1 1SA   Tel 071-821 7113

Price Band	££–£££
Credit Cards	Access, Visa
Bathrooms	Private and shared
Television	In rooms and lounge
Breakfast	English
Telephone	In rooms
Parking	Difficult

Hamilton House is slightly larger than the average B&B and, perhaps because it boasts a bar and restaurant as well as a lift, has more of a hotel "feel" than most in this book, while retaining the essential friendliness of a Bed and Breakfast. This is ensured by the manager, a delightful lady from Italy, who, professional to her fingertips, greets all her regular guests by name and often slips a bottle of wine or bunch of flowers into the room of a visiting honeymoon or wedding anniversary couple. The hallway is cosily panelled and bedrooms comfortable although smallish, with fairly stereotyped decor.

The restaurant serves very reasonably priced evening meals, making Hamilton House popular with business people and lone travellers, who do not always feel like venturing out to a restaurant on their own. For those wishing to make a reservation here, reduced rates are often available at week-ends.

Travel Instructions: *Train, underground or bus to* **Victoria.** *From the station forecourt turn left along Buckingham Palace Road and take the first left, Eccleston Bridge, leading into Belgrave Road. You will find Hamilton House on the right-hand side, just on the corner of Warwick Way.*

Harcourt House

50 Ebury Street
London
SW1W 0LU   Tel 071-730 2722

Price Band	££
Credit Cards	Amex
Bathrooms	Private and shared
Television	In rooms
Breakfast	English
Telephone	Public
Parking	Difficult

A shiny black door with polished brass plates and knocker welcome one to Harcourt House. Even the black railings around the area have been tipped in gold and there are flower boxes on the window sills. The interior of the house is light and airy and everything is spotlessly clean. The dining room is furnished with many ornaments and paintings and is more like a family's sitting room than a restaurant. The windows on the front have double-glazing.

It is run by a friendly young lady from Portugal who also speaks Spanish and Italian.

Travel Instructions: *Underground or BR to* **Victoria.** *Make your way to the front of the Grosvenor Hotel which stands on the side of the station. Opposite you will see Lower Belgrave Street. Walk along here and turn left into Ebury Street. Harcourt House is on the right.*

James House

108 Ebury Street
London
SW1W 9OD   Tel 071-730 7338

Price Band	££
Credit Cards	None
Bathrooms	Shared
Television	In rooms
Breakfast	English
Telephone	Public
Parking	Difficult

James House is owned and managed by the son and daughter-in-law of the owners of Cartref House (page 00) who plan to decorate it on similar lines. Already the breakfast room is cosy and charming with a fine collection of Ironstone tea and coffee pots, and further plans include refurbishing the bedrooms which are currently plain and simple, with tea/coffee making facilities and fresh-looking duvets.

The owners live in the flat below and have three small children which gives a real family feel to James House. A good B&B which will get better.

Travel Instructions: *Underground or British Rail to* **Victoria,** *turn left out of the station forecourt into Buckingham Palace Road which you cross and any right hand turning takes you into Ebury Street.*

Lewis House

111 Ebury Street
London
SW1 9QU   Tel 071-730 2094

Price Band	££–£££
Credit Cards	None
Bathrooms	Mainly shared
Television	In rooms
Breakfast	English
Telephone	Public
Parking	Difficult

Lewis House was first opened as a B&B by the parents of Sir Noel Coward, the legendary playwright, composer and entertainer, who lived here from 1917 to 1930. Understandably a great deal is made of this fact in the decor, including a plaque in the entrance hall and much memorabilia in the breakfast room. Otherwise Lewis House is a good average B&B, pleasantly decorated if a little expensive. Note there is no central heating.

Travel Instructions: *Underground or train to* **Victoria,** *turn left out of the station forecourt into Buckingham Palace Road. Cross, and any right-hand turning takes you into Ebury Street. Lewis House is on the left-hand side.*

Melita House

35 Charlwood Street
London
SW1V 2DU   Tel 071-828 0471/
                  834 1387
                  Fax 071-630 8905

Price Band	£
Credit Cards	Visa
Bathrooms	Mainly shared. Some private showers only.
Television	Lounge and in rooms (meter)
Breakfast	English
Telephone	Public
Parking	Difficult

Melita House has been providing spotless, budget-priced accommodation for visitors during the last fifteen years. Further improvements are planned to the bedrooms, most of which are large by London standards, especially the family rooms. Italian owned, the atmosphere is cosy and welcoming and reductions are available for children. The family also own one of Victoria's most popular restaurants, Mario and Toni's, nearby.

Travel Instructions: *Underground to* **Pimlico.** *Turning right, walk along Tachbrook Street and Charlwood Street is the second left. You will see Melita House on the right, after crossing Belgrave Road.*

Morgan Guest House ══════

120 Ebury Street
London
SW1W 9QQ   Tel 071-730 8442

Price Band	££
Credit Cards	Access, Visa
Bathrooms	Shared
Television	In rooms
Breakfast	English
Telephone	Public
Parking	Difficult

The Morgan Guest House is a very typical London B&B – with one nice exception: the management provides hairdryers in all the rooms, a luxury normally only found in the more expensive hotels. The bedrooms are comfortable, some retaining their elegant Victorian fireplaces. The main feature of the breakfast room is its modern brick fireplace and mantelpiece with various china ornaments. Through the window one sees purple and white heather in a well-placed window box.

A good B&B, especially convenient for Victoria Coach Station which is just two minutes' walk away.

Travel Instructions: *Underground or BR (train) to* **Victoria.** *Make your way to the Grosvenor Hotel and walk up Lower Belgrave Street which lies opposite it. Turn left into Ebury Street and walk a few minutes more. Morgan Guest House is on your right.*

Olympic House Hotel ══════

115 Warwick Way
London
SW1V 4JD   Tel 071-828 0757
                  071-821 1927

Price Band	££
Credit Cards	None
Bathrooms	Some shared; some rooms with private shower
Television	In rooms
Breakfast	English
Telephone	Public
Parking	Difficult

The Olympic House has just been completely refurbished, so everything is new and fresh. A new pine staircase has been made in the centre of the house and several of the bedrooms have their own little balconies. Flowers and plants abound. Bedrooms are small, plain and comfortable. The owners are a hard-working Polish couple with a friendly, relaxed attitude towards their guests. A good little B&B in a fairly quiet street.

Travel Instructions: *Underground or BR to* **Victoria.** *Walk along Buckingham Palace Road in the direction of the Coach Station. Opposite the Coach Station turn left over Elizabeth Bridge which runs into St. George's Drive. Walk past the Elizabeth Hotel and turn right into Warwick Way. The Olympic House is on the right.*

Note: *It is sometimes necessary to collect one's keys just across the road at No.134.*

Pyms Hotel ══════

118 Ebury Street
London
SW1W 9QQ   Tel 071-730 4986

Price Band	£££
Credit Cards	Access, Visa
Bathrooms	Shared
Television	In rooms
Breakfast	English
Telephone	Public
Parking	Difficult

Just five minutes' walk from Victoria Station, Pyms is a super little B&B run by a friendly Japanese lady. It's just the place for Japanese guests who are not too familiar with the English language, but naturally everyone is welcome.

The bedrooms and dining room are all freshly painted and sun streams through the windows. In the entrance hall is a charming little Edwardian wash stand, complete with china bowl.

Prices are on the high side, so it is worth asking whether any special rates are available.

Travel Instructions: *Underground to Victoria. Walk along Buckingham Palace Road in the direction of the Coach Station. Turn right into Elizabeth Street and then left into Ebury Street. You will see Pyms on your right.*

Richmond House Hotel ═══

38B Charlwood Street
London
SW1V 2DX   Tel 071-834 4577

Price Band	£
Credit Cards	None
Bathrooms	Shared
Television	In rooms
Breakfast	English
Telephone	Public
Parking	Difficult

The Richmond House is a small value-for-money B&B run by an English gentleman. Bedrooms are plain and comfortable, all fitted with hairdryers and tea and coffee-making facilities. The diningroom is decorated with a series of watercolours painted by a friend of the manager and depicting various London landmarks such as Battersea Power Station. Most of the guests who stay here return year after year and include a group of loyal civil servants.

Travel Instructions: *Underground to Pimlico. There are various exits, so ask someone to point you in the direction of Belgrave Road and walk along there until you come to Charlwood Street on the left. Richmond House Hotel is on the corner.*

Sir Gar House Hotel ═══

131 Ebury Street
London
SW1W 9QU   Tel 071-730 9378

Price Band	££
Credit Cards	None
Bathrooms	Mainly private
Television	In rooms
Breakfast	English
Telephone	Public
Parking	Difficult

The Sir Gar is one of the best B&B's in Ebury Street. On our visit in 1989, a total refurbishment programme was nearing completion. One enters through a beautiful glass and wooden door, painted in Trafalgar blue and white and with brass knockers etc into an attractive pale blue and white hall, hung with an antique chandelier.

A glance at the freshly painted bedrooms brought a smile to our eyes: everything, but everything matches. A design based on a blue and beige stripe is to be seen not only on duvet covers and curtains, but also on the tea tray (all rooms have tea and coffee-making facilities) and, of all places, on the waste-paper bin! This theme is carried through into the dining room where the owner herself has covered the chairs with the same material as the tablecloths.

Unusually for a central London B&B, guests are invited to sit out in the small garden to the rear on sunny days.

If you needs must stay in Victoria, you can do no better than make the Sir Gar your resting place.

Travel Instructions: *Underground or British Rail to Victoria. On leaving the station, walk along the Buckingham Palace Road past the Grosvenor Hotel and turn right into Eccleston Street. Then turn left into Ebury Street and you will soon see the Sir Gar on your left.*

Westminster House Hotel

96 Ebury Street
London
SW1 9QD   Tel 071-730 4302

Price Band	££
Credit Cards	None
Bathrooms	Private and shared
Television	In rooms
Breakfast	English
Telephone	Public
Parking	Difficult

The Westminster House is one of the many plain and comfortable B&B's in Ebury Street having pleasantly decorated rooms, all fitted with tea and coffee-making facilities. It is also one of the closest to Victoria Station – a five-minute walk – so ideal for visitors with an early departure from Gatwick.

Travel Instructions: *Underground or BR to Victoria. There are numerous exits from the station, so it is best to ask for Buckingham Palace Road and walk along it in the direction of the Coach Station until you come to Eccleston Street on your right. Walk along Eccleston Street and then turn left into Ebury Street. The Westminster House is on the right.*

Windermere Hotel

142 Warwick Way
London
SW1V 4JE   Tel 071-834 5163/
                 5480

Price Band	£££
Credit Cards	Visa
Bathrooms	Private
Television	In rooms
Breakfast	English
Telephone	In rooms
Parking	Difficult

The Windermere is small yet stylish, making it a great find for discerning visitors. Large windows in this corner building allow in plenty of light. Bedrooms are comfortable and well-furnished and the breakfast room unusually attractive. French doors open onto a tiny, whitewashed patio and tables are covered with pink tablecloths and set with pretty rose-patterned bone china.

An unusual feature for a B&B is room service of teas, coffees and sandwiches any time from 10a.m. to 10p.m. – a real touch of luxury!

The owner enjoys contact with his guests and normally serves the breakfast himself in order to have a chat with them and ensure they are enjoying their stay. Windermere is a deservedly popular B&B, so visitors should reserve well in advance to avoid disappointment.

Travel Instructions: *Underground or train to Victoria and from the station forecourt turn left into Buckingham Palace Road. Take the first left, Belgrave Road, then the first right – Hugh Street. Walk the entire length of this street, turn left at the end and you will see Windermere Hotel on the corner.*

MAPS. The maps in *London's Best Bed & Breakfast Hotels* will give readers an indication of where places are – but since they are largely diagrammatic they cannot be precise or detailed.

We strongly recommend that readers use one of the easily available and inexpensive London Street Guides or Maps obtainable in bookstalls, kiosks and bookshops from such publishers as Geographer's A-Z, Yellow Pages, Geographia, Bartholomew's and Robert Nicholson. Maps are also available from the London Tourist Board and London Transport.

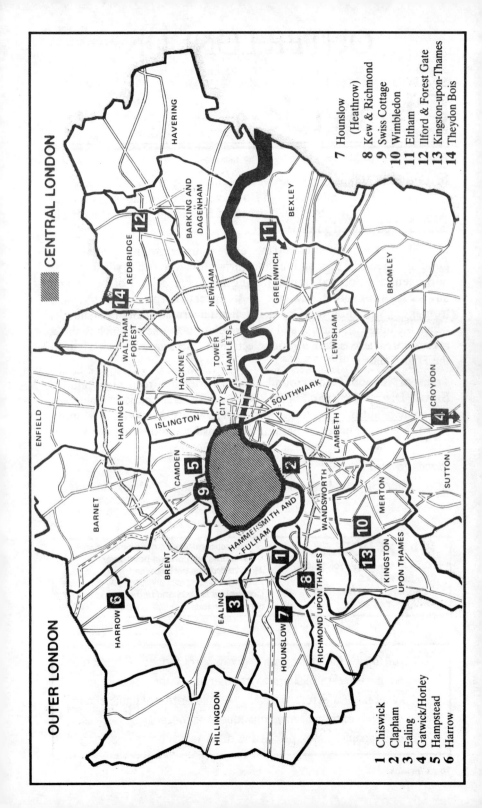

OUTER LONDON

CENTRAL LONDON

1 Chiswick
2 Clapham
3 Ealing
4 Gatwick/Horley
5 Hampstead
6 Harrow

7 Hounslow
   (Heathrow)
8 Kew & Richmond
9 Swiss Cottage
10 Wimbledon
11 Eltham
12 Ilford & Forest Gate
13 Kingston-upon-Thames
14 Theydon Bois

HAVERING

BEXLEY

REDBRIDGE

NEWHAM

GREENWICH

BROMLEY

WALTHAM FOREST

HACKNEY

TOWER HAMLETS

LEWISHAM

ENFIELD

HARINGEY

ISLINGTON

CITY

SOUTHWARK

CROYDON

BARNET

CAMDEN

LAMBETH

SUTTON

BRENT

HAMMERSMITH AND FULHAM

WANDSWORTH

MERTON

KINGSTON UPON THAMES

HARROW

EALING

HOUNSLOW

RICHMOND UPON THAMES

HILLINGDON

BARKING AND DAGENHAM

Chiswick

In Chiswick, situated to the west of London, the town meets the countryside. From the busy High Road, with its usual shops, banks and restaurants, run quiet tree-lined streets of Edwardian houses standing in flowery, well-tended gardens.

Only about twenty minutes into the centre by underground, Chiswick is a popular residential area and suitable for visitors who, while wishing to be fairly centrally located, are searching for some degree of peace and quietness. Probably Chiswick's most attractive spot is its riverside frontage at Strand-on-the-Green; a delightful stretch of Georgian houses which includes two ancient and very popular pubs, one of which is also a restaurant. There is, too, a good selection of restaurants and wine bars in the High Road.

Transport is good. Underground stations Turnham Green and Stamford Brook (District Line) and buses serve both central London (Route 88) and some beautiful spots to the west such as Kew Gardens and Hampton Court. Motorists have few parking problems here and Heathrow airport can be reached by car in less than twenty minutes.

Places to Visit
Kew Bridge Steam Museum   Hogarth's House   Chiswick House

BROOK HOTEL
50/54 Stamford Brook Road
London W6 0XL
Telephone: 081-743 2000
Fax: 081-743 6622

- Spacious, comfortable accommodation
- Most rooms with private bathrooms
- TV in bedrooms and lounge
- Parking
- Convenient for bus and underground to central London

Badger House

1 Airedale Avenue
London
W4 2NW   Tel 081-995 9754

Price Band	£
Credit Cards	None
Bathrooms	Shared
Television	In rooms
Breakfast	Continental (see below)
Telephone	Public
Parking	On street, plus 2 garages for guests' use

Although only moments from bustling Chiswick High Road, Badger House has the "Country" feel which one would expect from its name; a feeling enhanced by a really beautiful garden, both back and front.

Prints of the gentle little animal after which it is named adorn the hall and stairway, which are pleasantly decorated as are the good-sized bedrooms, all of which have tea/coffee-makers and fridges. Breakfast is a "Do-it-Yourself" affair with rolls, orange juice etc. supplied daily – a good choice for late risers! Badger House offers spotless cleanliness and a warm welcome at extremely competitive prices – Recommended.

Travel Instructions: *Underground to **Stamford Brook**. Turn right along Goldhawk Road and right again at Chiswick High Road. Airedale Avenue is across the road, the fourth turning on the left.*

Bedford Park House Hotel

57 Esmond Road
London
W4 1LG   Tel 081-747 0198

Price Band	££
Credit Cards	Access, Visa
Bathrooms	Private
Television	In rooms
Breakfast	English
Telephone	Payphone (Cardphone)
Parking	In forecourt

Bedford Park House Hotel stands in a quiet, leafy road in the most attractive part of Chiswick.

Colour schemes are light and pleasing while the bedrooms, which must be among the most spacious London has to offer, are equipped with tea/coffee-making facilities and fridges. Many also have sofas, armchairs and coffee tables and are more like suites than mere bedrooms. The delightful breakfast room leads onto a paved garden. Here, unusually for London, dinner is also served. Guests may relax here before, or after, a day's sightseeing.

Enthusiastic new management plan many further improvements to this lovely B&B which is definitely among West London's top ten – highly recommended.

Travel Instructions: *Underground to Turnham Green. Walk diagonally to the right across the Green to South Parade. Esmond Road is the third turning on the right. Note: this is a longish walk with luggage but taxis are usually available.*

Brook Hotel

50/54 Stamford Brook Road
London
W6 0XL   Tel 081-743 2000

Price Band	£££
Credit Cards	Visa
Bathrooms	Private (except two singles)
Television	In rooms and lounge
Breakfast	English
Telephone	In rooms
Parking	Easy, in forecourt and street

The creeper-covered facade of the Brook Hotel is instantly appealing to any visitors looking for a place to stay that is a blend of town and country. Formed of two houses skilfully knocked into one, there is a spacious square entrance hall from which twin staircases lead up to the comfortable bedrooms.

The charming, relaxed owners actually live next door and the many paintings, ornaments and well-chosen antiques bear witness to a lifetime of loving collecting. Carpeting throughout is in an unusual tartan that is both attractive and practical.

The breakfast room is a happy place to start the day. Pine furnishings, colourful tiled floor and bright china – French doors from both here and the lounge open on to the patio, where a fountain plays, and beyond is a lovely garden which guests are welcome to use. In the cosy bar visitors help themselves to drinks and write down what they have taken – a nice touch – teas, coffees and snacks also available. The use of a fax machine is an added attraction for business visitors. On a personal note I was once lucky enough to spend a night at the Brook and found it quite outstanding in all respects. Highly recommended.

Travel Instructions: *Underground to Stamford Brook, turn left along Goldhawk Road and sharp left at Charlotte's Wine Bar into Stamford Brook Road. The hotel is just three minutes' walk along, facing a small park.*
By car *from central London: take the main Bayswater road, continuing along Holland Park Avenue to the roundabout by the Kensington Hilton Hotel, straight on through Shepherd's Bush and at Charlotte's it is the right-hand fork. This is also the route of the **88 Bus** which has a stop right outside the Brook and is almost a sightseeing tour, travelling right through central London and passing most of the major sights.*

Elliott (Private) Hotel

62 Elliott Road
London
W4 1PE   Tel 081-995 9794

Price Band	£
Credit Cards	None
Bathrooms	Shared
Television	None
Breakfast	English
Telephone	Payphone
Parking	On street and one garage

The Elliott was originally two Victorian cottages which have been knocked into one to form this simple, spotless Guest House, now owned by a friendly Polish gentleman and his Spanish wife. Between them, they speak no less than eight languages!

Room rates are very reasonable, making this a good choice for budget-minded visitors, especially in summer, when the roses rambling over both back and front of the house are covered in bloom and form the focus of many a visitor's camera. An adjacent large park and seven tennis courts make this a good spot for sports enthusiasts and families.

Travel Instructions: *Underground to Turnham Green. Cross the road in front of the station and walk diagonally across the Green to the left and you will see the Elliott, which is painted white, on your left. Just two minutes' walk.*

Fouberts

162 Chiswick High Road
London
W4   Tel 081-995 6743

Price Band	££
Credit Cards	Visa
Bathrooms	Shared
Television	Lounge
Breakfast	Continental; English extra
Telephone	Public
Parking	Difficult

Those with fond recollections of Paris, Rome, or other continental cities cannot do better than make a bee-line for Fouberts.

Situated in bustling Chiswick High Road, with an enormous plane tree right outside, the building consists of a charming cafe/bar on the ground floor; downstairs is a wine bar (discounts for guests) and upstairs the fresh and simple rooms are spacious and tastefully decorated.

Breakfast is taken in the cafe/bar where the Italian owner is always to be found, chatting to customers and making endless cups of delicious Cappuchino. Definitely a bit of the continent in London!

Travel Instructions: *Underground to Turnham Green. Turn left out of the station and walk to the traffic lights. Turn left again – this is the High Road and Fouberts is on the left. About 5 minutes' walk.*

St Peter's Hotel

407 Goldhawk Road
London
W6 0SA   Tel 081-741 4239

Price Band	££
Credit Cards	All
Bathrooms	Private and shared.
Television	In rooms
Breakfast	English
Telephone	Public
Parking	Unmetered in street behind hotel

St Peters, standing on the corner of Goldhawk Road and Chiswick High Road, was totally refurbished during 1989 when the attractive French restaurant which fills the ground floor was first opened. Bedrooms, though small, are well-kept and have light colour schemes.

NOTE: There are no family rooms.

Travel Instructions: *Underground to Stamford Brook. Turn right out of the station and you will see St Peters on the opposite side of the road.*

Clapham

Ten years ago Clapham was somewhat of a run-down area. Today it is one of the great enclaves of what the English now term "Yuppies". A Yuppie is a young urban professional person on his/her way up . . . ! That is to say, there has been a proliferation of health food shops, expensive gift shops, delicatessens and restaurants, and the 19th and early 20th century houses have been renovated to a high standard and adorned with ruched curtains and flower boxes.

Clapham has three tube stations (only 15 minutes to Leicester Square) and plenty of ordinary shops. Its centrepiece is the Common which stretches almost a mile from one side to the other and which is bounded by the South Circular Road. The A23 road to Gatwick is litle more than a mile away, so this is an especially good location for visitors with cars, whilst at the same time being very convenient for public transport.

Places to Visit

Very little in the way of tourist attractions in Clapham. Either take a stroll over the extensive Common (at its best in autumn) or take the tube into the city centre.

Girl Leaning on a Windowsill *Rembrandt*

DULWICH PICTURE GALLERY

London's most perfect gallery
The Guardian

1987 National Art Collection Fund Award for Education
1988 Museums of the Year Awards, Best Fine Art Museum
1989 European Museum of the Year Awards, Special Commendation

Open Tuesday to Sunday

Dulwich Picture Gallery

College Road, London SE21 7BG
Recorded Information 081-693 8000

Complaints

We very much hope that you will be happy with the B&B you choose from this guide. However, should you have any cause for complaint or suggestions for improvement, please do not hesitate to pass them on to the owner or manager, who will usually be only too keen to put things right.

If you have a serious complaint which cannot be settled on the spot, you should contact the London Tourist Board (071-730 3450) and you should also write to us. We will follow up all such complaints but we regret that we cannot act as intermediaries or on your behalf nor can we or the Publishers accept responsibility for any of the services or accommodation described.

Edwards Guest House ═══

91 Abbeville Road
Clapham Common
London
SW4 9JL   Tel 071-622 6347

Price Band	£
Credit Cards	None
Bathrooms	Shared
Television	Usually available in room on request
Breakfast	English
Telephone	Public
Parking	Unrestricted parking on street

The Edwards Guest House is situated in one of Clapham's nicest "Yuppie" streets. Abbeville Road is a long elegant road, part shops (there is even a tiny Post Office) and restaurants and part residential – ideal for holiday-makers. The Edwards is run by a friendly Malaysian lady and whilst the rooms are fairly plain, there are odd pieces of rattan furniture and an antique Malaysian vase which give it that charm of which we spoke in the introduction. The bedrooms are light and quiet on both the front and the back of the house. The dining room is small and looks onto the tiny back garden. The front garden is a mass of colour, with a series of chimney pots on one side containing a glorious mixture of pinks and blues. An excellent value-for-money B&B, one of the very cheapest in London. Bookings of more than one night, please.

Travel Instructions: *Underground to **Clapham Common**. On leaving the station, walk along Clapham Common South Side and turn left into Cresent Lane. Abbeville Road is then the third road on the right and the Edwards Guest House is a short way along on the right (10 minutes from the station).*

Ealing

═══════════════════════════════

Ealing is a large borough, mainly residential, some 30 minutes by tube west of the city centre. Its focus is the new shopping mall and adjacent shops and station (Ealing Broadway). There are many large houses and leafy streets and it is possible to find very reasonably priced accommodation in the area. Just five minutes' walk from the Broadway is the delightful Walpole Park with a fine house, Pitshanger Manor, standing on its edge.

Ealing is well-served by the underground: both District and Central Lines terminate there and it is only a short bus ride (No. 65) to some of London's most interesting attractions beside the River Thames (see below). Parking is very easy, so it is an excellent location for visitors with cars.

Places to Visit

Kew Bridge Steam Museum
Kew Gardens

The Musical Museum
Pitshanger Manor Museum

Mrs J.A. Clements ═══════

17 Madeley Road
Ealing
London
W5 2LA

Tel 081-998 5222
Fax 081-994 9144
Telex 933859

Price Band	££–£££
Credit Cards	None
Bathrooms	Private and shared
Television	In lounge
Breakfast	English
Telephone	Public
Parking	Private parking on forecourt

The most striking characteristic of Mrs Clements' B&B is the beautiful woodwork, some of which is original pine (as in the carefully restored doors) and some of which is maple as in the modern dining room floor. The dining room is in fact combined with an attractive open-plan kitchen, giving that wonderful feeling of spaciousness which is so lacking in most London B&B's. Guests are invited to help themselves to tea and coffee from the kitchen whenever they wish.

Spaciousness is equally the hallmark of the luxurious bedrooms. These are decorated with expensive curtains, gilt mirrors etc. and some of the bathrooms (in white marble-effect tiles and gold) are better than those of a 5-star hotel! And just in case you are imagining that Mrs Clements is a little on the stuffy side, let me assure you that I spotted bundles of children's toys tumbling over the dining room floor, and that the good lady herself welcomes guests in her jeans – a super combination of elegance and informality. Strongly recommended.

Travel Instructions: *Underground to Ealing Broadway. Turn right out of station and right again into Madeley Road. Mrs Clements' is just a couple of minutes walk along on the left.*

White House ═══════

9 Woodville Gardens
Ealing
London
W5 2LG

Tel 081-998 9208

Price Band	£
Credit Cards	None
Bathrooms	Shared
Television	In lounge
Breakfast	English
Telephone	Public
Parking	Unrestricted on street

The White House is a large, handsome, detached house with a white balcony, unusual "Dutch Tile" effect facade and paintwork picked out in yellow. It stands in a very quiet residential street. The bedrooms are large and the lounge and breakfast room are filled with plants (including an enormous palm in the lounge), displays of china, silk cushions, etc. French windows lead from the breakfast room into a large secluded garden with table and chairs for the use of guests.

Prices are very low for London – an excellent value-for-money B&B.

Travel Instructions: *Underground to Ealing Broadway. Turn right out of the tube and first right into Madeley Road. Turn left into Haven Lane and Woodville Gardens is then the first road on the right. Walk a little way along and you will come to the White House just past the junction of Westbury Road.*

Eltham

At first sight, Eltham, lying some 7 miles south east of central London, is no more than an average suburb with its High Street shops and residential side streets. However, closer inspection reveals a wealth of open spaces and two "jewels": Eltham Palace and Avery Hill Winter Garden.

Tucked away at the end of a leafy lane, Eltham Palace consists of the Great Hall built by Edward IV in 1480 (this is all that remains of the original palace), a mansion house erected in the 1930's and a series of low ruined walls, all surrounded by exquisite gardens and a moat.

Avery Hill Winter Garden, now part of a teachers' training college, is in fact a massive Victorian glass dome housing all sorts of exotic plants and trees: breadfruit, date palms, bananas etc, overlooking gardens and extensive playing fields.

Other open spaces include the Tarn which is a public park and bird sanctuary, Well Hall Park (opposite the station) and the Royal Blackheath Golf Course.

The great advantage of staying in Eltham is that it is only a couple of miles away from Greewich, one of London's most historic and most beautiful "villages" (see below for places to visit).

As I wandered around the streets in south east London seeking out B&B's (to my knowledge there are none in Greenwich itself) I thought how pleasant it would be to spend three or four days holiday solely in Eltham, Greenwich and the neighbouring village of Blackheath, without going near the centre of London.

Bus No 286 runs from Eltham via Blackheath to Greenwich. British Rail trains run from Eltham and New Eltham into Charing Cross in central London, approximately every half hour.

The A2 and A20 roads from the channel ports pass directly through Eltham and parking is easy, making it very convenient for drivers.

Places to Visit

Cutty Sark	Avery Hill Winter Garden
Eltham Palace	Greenwich Park
Old Royal Observatory	Royal Naval College
National Maritime Museum	Thames Barrier

Clevedun Hotel ═══════

503 Footscray Road
New Eltham
London
SE9 3UH   Tel 081-859 6215

Price Band	£
Credit Cards	Visa, Mastercard
Bathrooms	Shared
Television	In lounge and rooms
Breakfast	English
Telephone	Public
Parking	Private car park

The Clevedun Hotel has recently been taken over by the owners of the Meadow Croft Lodge half a mile away. Their standards are high and although this is already an excellent B&B, they plan to make further improvements.

The reception area is decorated with vases of flowers and leads directly into a welcoming dining room with pottery crockery and French windows opening onto a raised patio.

There is a comfortable lounge with deep red velvet curtains and traditional floral-patterned carpet. The bathrooms are tiled in blue and on the large side for London, whilst bedrooms are light and pretty and all have tea and coffee making facilities.

Prices are very reasonable for the standard of comfort: strongly recommended.

Travel Instructions: *British Rail from Charing Cross to New Eltham. Turn right out of the station approach and walk along Footscray Road for some ten minutes. You will find the Clevedun Hotel on your left at the junction of Chartwell Close.*

Meadow Croft Lodge ═══════

96-98 Southwood Road
New Eltham
London
SE9 3QS   Tel 081-859 1488

Price Band	£-££
Credit Cards	Visa
Bathrooms	Some shared; some rooms with private shower
Television	In lounge and rooms
Breakfast	English
Telephone	Public
Parking	Private car park

The owners of Meadow Croft Lodge, Stephanie and Trevor Powell, have called on the services of an interior designer in the refurbishment of this very welcoming B&B. The result is a refreshingly unusual colour scheme in apricot, white, grey and deep blues in the public areas, and the installation in the bedrooms of shelves, louvred doors and little niches in varnished pine. The picture is completed with flowery duvets and curtains. Tea and coffee-making facilities are available in all rooms.

Considering what an attractive B&B this is, prices are very modest.

Travel Instructions: *Take the British Rail train from Charing Cross to New Eltham (trains run every half hour). Turn right out of the station approach road and immediately right again into Southwood Road. Five minutes' walk will bring you to Meadow Croft Lodge on the right.*

Prices

We have sought to avoid the complicated symbols used in most guide books, retaining only one (£) to indicate the rates you may expect to pay. These are indicated thus:

£	Up to £32 Double/Twin Room – Up to £22 Single Room
££	£33–£45 Double/Twin Room – £23–£30 Single Room
£££	£46–£55 Double/Twin Room – £31–£40 Single Room
££££	£56–£70 Double/Twin Room – £41–£55 Single Room

(*Note:* Double = 1 large bed, Twin = 2 single beds)

These prices can, naturally, only form a general guideline, since they are subject to seasonal variations. **Always confirm prices when making a booking, and check that they include breakfast, VAT (tax) and service charges.**

Weston House

8 Eltham Green
Eltham
London
SE9 5LB

Tel 081-850 5191
081-850 5409

Price Band	££
Credit Cards	Visa
Bathrooms	Private and shared
Television	In rooms and lounge
Breakfast	English
Telephone	Public
Parking	Unrestricted on street

Weston House is a good, plain B&B in an area which has few places to stay. Situated right beside the South Circular Road (A205) and within a mile or two of the M20 and M2 which come in from Dover, it is ideally suited for drivers. With the proximity of the road in mind, light sleepers are advised to request a room at the back of the house. One of the rooms I saw was a cosy little double under the gables and overlooking a large garden which guests are encouraged to use.

Travel Instructions: Take a British Rail train from **Charing Cross** to **Eltham**. It is a good fifteen minute walk from the station, so take a taxi (minicab) when you arrive with luggage.

Yardley Court

18 Court Yard
Eltham
London
SE9 5PZ

Tel 081-850 1850

Price Band	££
Credit Cards	Access, Visa
Bathrooms	Private and shared
Television	In rooms and lounge
Breakfast	English
Telephone	Public
Parking	Private car park

An old brick house painted in blue and covered in ivy and Virginia creeper, Yardley Court gives one the feeling of being in the country although Eltham is quite a busy suburb. It has only nine bedrooms, all very prettily decorated, some with a little arch over the bed, others tucked in the attic under a skylight.

The dining room which rises a few feet above the garden is in the style of a conservatory, its long walls of glass allowing a maximum of sun and light to enter this lovely room. It is furnished with thick green carpet and a cane sofa and chairs. Breakfast at Yardley Court is recommended by Egon Ronay: the best B&B for miles around.

Travel Instructions: British Rail from **Charing Cross** to **Eltham**. Turn left out of the station, walk along Well Hall Road, cross over traffic lights at junction of Eltham High Street and you will see Yardley Court on your right (5 minutes' walk).

Hampstead and Golders Green

Hampstead and its Heath, standing on a hill to the north of the capital, has an identity all its own which is reflected in the many famous people from the world of the theatre, literature and politics who have chosen to make their homes there. The great actress Sarah Siddons had an adorable house overlooking the Heath, while writers John Galsworthy, D. H. Lawrence and Edgar Wallace all lived here at some time. Although these houses cannot be visited, it adds great interest to a stroll through Hampstead to see the blue plaques identifying them and to imagine lifestyles in days gone by. Hampstead centre, around the station, has become somwewhat over-developed in recent years although strenuous efforts by the local Preservation Society have prevented too many ugly shop-fronts and have helped retain much of its character. This can only be appreciated by exploring some of the side roads, many of which are as charming as their names: Church Row with its beautiful 18th century houses, Holly Hill where stands the Holly Bush, one of London's few remaining unmodernised pubs, and pretty Well Walk.

A longer walk, up Heath Street and past the pond, leads one to the glorious Heath, 825 acres of park and woodland, beloved of walkers, picnickers, children, dogs and those just wishing to escape from the city centre to breathe fresh air and re-charge their batteries. At the top of the hill stands Kenwood House, a fine 18th century mansion, furnished in the style of the period and containing magnificent paintings by Gainsborough and Reynolds, two of that century's foremost artists. In the grounds of Kenwood House, beside the lake, concerts of classical music are held on Saturday evenings during the summer months. Even allowing for our imperfect climate these are a lovely experience and well worthwhile for the visitor. Warm up afterwards right opposite at the Spaniards Inn, built in the 16th century and a favourite drinking place ever since with many of Hampstead's intelligentsia.

As well as pubs, Hampstead has an excellent selection of coffee shops and several outstanding restaurants, notably the enchanting Villa Bianca tucked away in Perrins Court and serving some of the best Italian food outside Italy.

Just one Underground stop north of Hampstead, or a short walk across Golders Hill Park, is Golders Green, totally different in character from its neighbour, being a modern suburb. Nothing in Golders Green dates back further than the beginning of this century and the atmosphere is conventional but clean, pleasant and well laid-out with good shops (including an attractive new shopping mall), restaurants and a fair selection of B&B's, unlike Hampstead which, sadly, has only very few.

Transport is by Underground – Hampstead or Golders Green (both Northern Line) and good bus services to Golders Green. Hampstead, being on a hill, cannot take double-decker buses although service 210, which starts from Golders Green station, stops right outside Kenwood House and is useful for those who do not fancy a climb!

Places to Visit (all in Hampstead)

Fenton House

Freud Museum

Keat's House

Kenwood House

Frognal Lodge Hotel ══════

14 Frognal Gardens
London
NW3 6UX

Tel 071-435 8238
Telex 25477
SHAINA G

Price Band	££–£££
Credit Cards	Access, Visa
Bathrooms	Private and shared
Television	In rooms and lounge
Breakfast	English
Telephone	In rooms
Parking	Usually possible in street

Frognal Lodge is situated immediately off one of Hampstead's most delightful streets – Church Row. 1989 has seen the total redecoration of the interior and the installation of a new lift. The bedrooms have been upgraded so that they now all have hairdryers and Sky TV and those rooms with private facilities also have tea and coffee-making facilities and trouser presses.

Lying on an exclusive residential street, Frognal Lodge is an ideal location for visitors seeking a quiet room. However, the greatest attraction of the Frognal Lodge is the size of its en-suite bedrooms – they are the largest I have ever seen anywhere in London!

Travel Instructions: *Underground to* **Hampstead.** *Walk just a few yards down Heath Street and you*

will find Church Row on your right. Frognal Gardens is the first road on the right off Church Row.

Golders Green Hotel ══════

147-149 Golders Green Road
London
NW11 9BN

Tel 081-458 7127

Price Band	££–£££
Credit Cards	Access, Amex, Visa
Bathrooms	Private
Television	In rooms
Breakfast	Continental
Telephone	In rooms
Parking	In forecourt

The Golders Green Hotel is a well-furnished, immaculately kept and altogether excellent place for Jewish visitors. Bedrooms are comfortable with pleasing colour schemes and the breakfast room is light and attractive. *Please Note:* This is a strictly Kosher hotel and licensed by the Beth Din of the Federation of Synagogues.

Travel Instructions: *Underground to* **Golders Green.** *Turn right on leaving the station, crossing the busy Finchley Road you will find yourself in Golders Green Road – the hotel is on the left, just past the shops.*

Hampstead Village Guest House

2 Kemplay Road
Hampstead
London
NW3 1SY   Tel 071-435 8679

Price Band	££
Credit Cards	None
Bathrooms	Shared
Television	In rooms
Breakfast	English (reduction of approximately £3 for visitors not wishing to take breakfast)
Telephone	Public
Parking	On street

It is difficult to do justice to the Hampstead Village Guest House. On reflection, I feel that it is the best B&B I have seen in the London area. Its charm lies not only in the fact that the double-fronted Victorian house itself is exquisite and retains many original features, but in the fact that the rooms are crammed full of personal belongings: books, records, a wicker-work basket etc., and that a cat and a dog are integral parts of the household. So rarely in London B&B's does one come across such trust which gives so comforting a feeling of security.

In the dining room is a huge pine dresser, again crammed with cups, plates etc. and to its left an old-fashioned marble-topped sideboard. As they take breakfast, guests look out over pots of red geraniums standing on a garden table.

The bedrooms are large and differ in style from one to the other. Most have natural pine floors and antique furniture. Particularly attractive is the "Blue" room which really needs to be seen to be appreciated. All rooms have tea and coffee-making facilities and hairdryers and most have fridges and trouser presses. Unbelievably, the charge for a double room in this wonderful establishment is £38 per night (1990 prices).

Please note that smoking is not permitted.

Travel Instructions: *Underground to* **Hampstead.** *On leaving the station walk down Hampstead High Street and turn left after some five minutes into Pilgrim's Lane. Kemplay Road is then the first street on the left and the Hampstead Village Guest House is the first house on the right.*

La Gaffe

107 Heath Street
London
NW3 6SS   Tel 071-435 8965/66/67

Price Band	£££
Credit Cards	Access, Amex, Diners, Visa
Bathrooms	Private
Television	In rooms
Breakfast	Continental
Telephone	In rooms
Parking	Difficult

Definitely a place of character. One of a row of houses built in 1730, La Gaffe consists, on the ground floor, of a typical Italian restaurant and a lively cafe/bar. From there a staircase leads past a flower-decked roof terrace to the bedrooms which are smallish and simply furnished but, nevertheless, full of charm. Each room is named after an artist with prints of his work adorning the walls, or a theme such as the Campari Room which gives a clue to the owners' favourite drink!

Mr Bernardo speaks four languages and, as he says. "loves people". Visitors return again and again as much for the atmosphere as for the area.

On our last visit we were pleased to find that new double-glazed windows had been installed and that the construction of new bathrooms was well under way.

Travel Instructions: *Underground to* **Hampstead.** *Turn right on leaving the station and just keep walking uphill for about five minutes. La Gaffe is on the left.*

Regal Guest House

170 Golders Green Road
London
NW11 9BY   Tel 081-455 7025

Price Band	££
Credit Cards	Access, Amex, Visa
Bathrooms	Private and shared
Television	In rooms
Breakfast	English
Telephone	Public
Parking	In forecourt: 4 cars only

The Regal Guest House, set well back from the main road, is friendly, welcoming and spotless. The pleasant well-furnished breakfast room has enormous windows for maximum light and "anything you want" is served at breakfast time. Bedrooms and bathrooms are pretty, with pleasing colour schemes and nice lighting. All beds have duvets.

Some departing guests reported that they wouldn't stay anywhere else in north London – enough said!

Travel Instructions: *Underground to Golders Green, turn right, cross over the roundabout and walk up Golders Green Road. The Regal is on the right-hand side, just past the shops.*

Harrow

Churchill and Byron, suburbia and commuters – this is Harrow, a definite two-part town.

Above the grassy, wooded banks of its famous hill rises the majestic spire of St. Mary's Church. Close by nestle the buildings of one of the most famous public schools in the world – Harrow School itself. The school numbers among its former pupils not only Churchill and Byron, but also a whole string of prime ministers, kings, archbishops and literary figures.

Harrow-on-the-Hill has a charming village atmosphere with narrow streets, good pubs and cottage-style gardens. Back on the "mainland" it is a different story . . . ! Here you will find thousands of the semi-detached houses surrounded by their neat little gardens which typify true suburbia. These houses owe their existence to the expansion between the wars of the Metropolitan Railway to Harrow. They are largely occupied by families, and most of the fathers travel by tube to work in the West End or City each day. Since the journey is very fast – approximately 30 minutes – and since its shopping facilities are excellent, Harrow is also a good spot for visitors with cars who are not prepared to risk the horrors of London's privatised clamping brigade!

Places to Visit

Harrow School
Headstone Manor
St. Mary's Church

Wembley Market
Wembley Stadium

Central Hotel ═══════════

6 Hindes Road
Harrow
Middlesex
HA1 1SJ   Tel 081-427 0893

Price Band	£–££
Credit Cards	Access, Visa
Bathrooms	Private and shared
Television	In rooms
Breakfast	English
Telephone	Public
Parking	Large car park

This is an absolutely spotless, family-run B&B. Bathrooms have fresh blue and white tiles and carpets look brand new, although we were told that they are twelve years old! The bedrooms are cosy with nice easy chairs and tea-making facilities tucked away in a little nook. Outside there are flower boxes on the windowsills and pots of lilies around the base of the bay.

Prices are on the low side for the area. Strongly recommended.

Travel Instructions: *Underground to Harrow Met. Walk down past a couple of little shops and turn right into College Road, then left into Station Road. Walk along this road past the Church of St. John the Baptist until you come to Hindes Road on your left. The Central Hotel is just around the corner on the left (10 minutes from the Underground).*

Hindes Hotel ═══════════

8 Hindes Road
Harrow
Middlesex
HA1 1SJ   Tel 081-427 7468

Price Band	£–££
Credit Cards	Access, Visa
Bathrooms	Private and shared
Television	In lounge and in rooms
Breakfast	English
Telephone	Public
Parking	In forecourt

The unusual feature of the Hindes Hotel is its pretty little breakfast room which has an open kitchen section at one end and little wooden tables and benches along the other. These are laid with bright blue mats and blue and white cups and plates. There is a terracotta tiled floor and a door onto the garden. Although the dining room might remind one of Switzerland or Italy, the owner is in fact an ambitious Sikh gentleman who hopes this year to add a two-storey extension and additional car-park to his establishment.

The bedrooms have modern white furniture and tea-making facilities. Those on the back are very quiet. A good value-for-money B&B in an area which has mainly two-star style hotels at twice the price.

Travel Instructions: *Underground to Harrow Met. Walk down past a couple of little shops and turn right into College Road, then left into Station Road. Walk along this road past the Church of St. John the Baptist until you come to Hindes Road on your left. The Hindes Hotel is just around the corner on the left (10 minutes from Underground).*

Marlborough Hill Guest House ═══════

90 Marlborough Hill
Harrow
Middlesex
HA1 1TY   Tel 081-427 0771

Price Band	£
Credit Cards	None
Bathrooms	Public
Television	In rooms
Breakfast	Continental, self-service
Telephone	There is no telephone for use of guests, but call box is close by
Parking	Unrestricted on street

The Marlborough Guest House is a very cheap, very plain B&B consisting of 6 tiny single rooms only. It is run by a friendly English couple whose guests are mainly business people who have been coming regularly for many years. However, they are always pleased to welcome tourists and students and their establishment is in a residential quarter, so it is also good for visitors requiring a quiet room.

Guests are invited to help themselves to breakfast, and to tea and coffee at any time, from a special counter on the first floor. An iron is also placed at their disposal.

Travel Instructions: *Either British Rail (from Euston) or Bakerloo Line to **Harrow and Wealdstone** (changing onto British Rail at **Queen's Park** if necessary). Exit by rear of station and walk along slip road, turning right at the end into Marlborough Hill. Five minutes' walk will bring you to Marlborough Hill Guest House which you will find on the left beside a pillar box. A sign above the door reads "Endeavour" (10 minutes from station).*

Rhondda Guest House ═══════

16 Harrow View
Harrow
Middlesex
HA1 1RG   Tel 081-427 5009

Price Band	££
Credit Cards	None
Bathrooms	Private and shared
Television	In rooms
Breakfast	English
Telephone	Public
Parking	Private car park

Beside the entrance door to the Rhondda Guest House is a sign which reads "On this site in 1897 nothing happened" – a clear indication that the owner of the establishment has a sense of humour . . . ! And indeed I was not disappointed as the door opened to reveal a highly bronzed gentleman in a dazzlingly white beach robe! He and his wife run one of Harrow's best B&B's. The bedrooms are decorated with imagination; they vary in style from one to the other; they have thick pile carpets and dainty wickerwork chairs. Above all, there is that wonderful feeling of *spaciousness* which is so lacking in most London B&B's.

There are tea and coffee-making facilities in all the rooms and windows are double-glazed. Non-smokers are preferred.

Very strongly recommended for visitors who are looking for that little bit of extra comfort at an affordable price. Reductions are available for bookings of more than 4 nights.

Travel Instructions: *Underground to **Harrow-on-the-Hill**. On leaving the station, turn left into College Road and then right into Headstone Road. This runs directly into Harrow View and you will find the Rhondda Guest House on the left (10 minutes' walk from the Tube).*

Ilford and Forest Gate

Ilford and Forest Gate are largely residential areas 6 miles or so to the east of the City. Clustered around Ilford Station are all the shops one finds in a busy High Street, whilst Valentine's Park and Wanstead Park are within easy walking distance. There is no Tube, but a simple change from the Central Line at Stratford onto British Rail will bring you to Forest Gate and Ilford in approximately 10 minutes. The bus No 25 goes from Victoria via Oxford Street and Holborn to Ilford, but is somewhat slower than the train. For drivers, the M11 passes right through Ilford and the M25 lies some 8 miles away.

There is little in the way of tourist attractions in the area: it is best to come into the centre.

Arran Guest House

7 Argyle Road
Ilford
Essex
IG1 3BH   Tel 081-478 3796

Price Band	£
Credit Cards	None
Bathrooms	Shared
Television	In rooms and lounge
Breakfast	English
Telephone	Public
Parking	Private car park

The Arran Guest House is run by the daughter of the owners of the Woodville Guest House which faces it on the other side of Argyle Road.

Like the Woodville, it is an exceptionally good B&B with a pretty dining room-cum-lounge with dark wooden tables and chairs and a pale lemon and white ceiling. It is one of the few B&B's to offer satellite TV.

Each bedroom has its own character with antique furniture dotted here and there and tea and coffee-making facilities being available. Note that bathrooms have showers rather than bathtubs.

Prices are very modest considering the standard of comfort. Strongly recommended.

Travel Instructions: *Take the Central Line to Stratford and change onto British Rail, alighting at Ilford. Turn left out of the station and left into York Road. Argyle Road is the second turning on the right and the Arran Guest House is on the left (approximately 5 minutes' walk).*

Conifers Guest House =====

5 Argyle Road
Ilford
Essex
IG1 3BH   Tel 081-478 0936

Price Band	£–££
Credit Cards	None
Bathrooms	Private and shared
Television	In rooms and in dining room
Breakfast	English
Telephone	Public
Parking	Private car park

The Conifers Guest House is another very good B&B in the cluster of better-than-average establishments at the southern end of Argyle Road.

The ground floor dining room has attractive round tables, a chandelier and a large bay window. Bedrooms are bright and have pretty flowery duvets and thick carpets. In line with the name "Conifers", a green colour scheme predominates throughout and is used to great advantage in the bathrooms which are tiled, carpeted and enormous by London standards!

Travel Instructions: *Take the Central Line to Stratford and change onto British Rail, alighting at Ilford. Turn left out of the station and left into York Road. Argyle Road is the second turning on the right and the Conifers Guest House is on the left (approximately 5 minutes' walk).*

McCreadie Hotel =====

357-363 Romford Road
Forest Gate
London
E7 8AA   Tel 081-555 8528

Price Band	£
Credit Cards	None
Bathrooms	Mostly shared, a few private
Television	In lounge and in a few rooms
Breakfast	English
Telephone	Public
Parking	Large private car park

The McCreadie Hotel is one of the very few really good B&B's we were able to find in East London. The majority of the B&B's in this area either take in homeless families or specialise in weekly terms for workers.

It is very definitely a family-run B&B and has a cosy lounge, the focal point of which is an intricately carved wooden bar imported by the owners themselves from Thailand.

There is a large dining room in which, as well as breakfast, an evening meal is available on Monday-Thursday inclusive at a price of around £6.

Bedrooms vary one from another. One of the larger rooms I saw had a huge bay window and a couple of easy chairs. The single which I saw, whilst not being large, was pleasant and had a pretty turquoise quilt etc.

Note that there are no bathtubs in this establishment, only showers.

Travel Instructions: *If you are coming by public transport from Central London, take the Central Line and make an easy change onto British Rail at Stratford and then alight at Forest Gate. Turn right out of the station and, after two minutes' walk, turn left into Romford Road. You will soon find the McCreadie Hotel on your left.*

Note that the bus No 25 (Victoria/Oxford Street/Holborn) stops right beside the McCreadie but that it is a rather slow means of transport. For drivers, the Romford Road is the A118 and the McCreadie is at the junction of Richmond Road.

Woodville Guest House

10 Argyle Road
Ilford
Essex
IG1 3BO   Tel 081-478 3779

Price Band	£
Credit Cards	None
Bathrooms	Shared
Television	In rooms and lounge
Breakfast	English
Telephone	Public
Parking	Private car park

After having spent a morning trailing around East London and finding nothing but B&B's which accommodate homeless families, I had the wonderful surprise of coming upon the Woodville Guest House.

For £28 (1990) a night for a double room, guests may enjoy the luxurious surroundings of an establishment which would cost at least twice the price in central London.

The Woodville is owned by a Scottish couple whose taste is impeccable. On entering, one's gaze is immediately drawn towards the delicate grey ceiling of the lounge with its elegant chandelier, and then towards the spacious dining room beyond.

A stag's head decorates the hall, bedrooms are furnished with antiques and floral duvets and bathrooms are carpeted, the whole being quite irresistible!

Note that bedrooms have tea and coffee-making facilities and that bathrooms have showers, not bathtubs.

Travel Instructions: *Take the Central Line to Stratford and change onto British Rail, alighting at Ilford. Turn left out of the station and left into York Road. Argyle Road is the second turning on the right and the Woodville is on the right (five minutes' walk from the station).*

York Hotel

8 York Road
Ilford
Essex
IG1 3AD   Tel 081-514 1166
                 081-478 8107

Price Band	£–££
Credit Cards	None
Bathrooms	Private and shared
Television	In rooms
Breakfast	English
Telephone	Public
Parking	Private

The York Hotel epitomises all that visitors to England expect to find in a good B&B.

It is run by an English couple who really do put their heart and soul into making the guests feel at home: they will get up at the crack of dawn if their "boys" require early breakfast and they will allow single girls to use a special bathroom which is out of bounds for the male populace. They also spend hours tending the garden, looking after the dogs and feeding a baby fox which creeps along their hedge at dusk!

The bedrooms are very attractive (the owners threaten re-decoration, though I was not able to find the slightest mark of wear and tear!), but it is the dining room which is the *pièce de résistance*. It's walls are completely covered with a vast assortment of plates: modern, antique, humorous and delicate. An evening meal is available in this dining room on Mondays to Thursdays inclusive. Bedrooms have tea and coffee-making facilities and alarm radios. Highly recommended.

Travel Instructions: *Take the Central Line to Stratford and change onto British Rail, alighting at Ilford. Turn left out of the station and left into York Road. You will soon see the York Hotel on the right (three minutes' walk from station).*

Kew and Richmond

Kew and Richmond lie on the River Thames some 40 minutes by tube west of the city centre. They are both fashionable residential areas with enormous family houses (a number of which date from the 17th and 18th centuries) and well-established gardens.

Kew is renowned the world over for its Botanical Gardens. For a small charge one may spend a glorious day exploring its 300 acres of woodland, lakes and flower plantations and, of course, its majestic glasshouses where the oppressive humidity and the lush, rampant vegetation conspire to transport one far away from London's grey skies . . . !

Richmond is also an area of wide open spaces: a beautiful walk up Richmond Hill, past the Star and Garter home for disabled seamen, brings one to the bare heathland of Richmond Park, once a royal hunting ground and still the home of some 600 freely roaming red and fallow deer. Below the hill lies the town of Richmond itself with a charming Victorian terracotta-faced theatre overlooking the Green, high-street shops, antique shops, and London's oldest bridge (1777) spanning the Thames. With Hampstead, Kew and Richmond rank amongst London's most delightful "villages". Transport to both from central London is via the District line.

Places to Visit

Ham House	Marble Hill House
Kew Gardens	Richmond Park
Orleans House	Richmond Theatre

The Bingham Hotel on Thames

61 Petersham Road
Richmond
Surrey
TW10 6UT   Tel 081-940 0902

Price Band	££££
Credit Cards	Access, Amex, Diners, Visa
Bathrooms	Private
Television	In rooms
Breakfast	English
Telephone	In rooms
Parking	Car park

The Bingham, as its name suggests, stands in an idyllic position with gardens sloping down to one of the most beautiful stretches of the Thames.

Many bedrooms have spectacular views as does the breakfast room, which is skilfully designed to place the maximum number of tables by its large windows. Public areas in this listed Georgian building have been recently refurbished with great taste: deep-pile carpets, William Morris wallpaper and lovely chandeliers. Charming, comfortable bedrooms all have tea/coffee makers and those in the front are double-glazed for extra quietness, while bathrooms are gleaming and inviting.

There is a small bar and excellent restaurant, with French doors opening onto the garden, which has recently been landscaped. The Bingham has all the luxury of a three-star hotel (at about half the price!) combined with the friendliness of a B&B. It's a place for that special occasion – perfect for a romantic week-end or the last night of vacation. Please note it is a long walk from Richmond station, see below.

Travel Instructions: *Underground or train to **Richmond** then taxi or bus 65 which stops right outside.*

The Coach and Horses

8 The Green
Kew, Richmond
Surrey
TW9 3BH   Tel 081-940 1208

Price Band	££
Credit Cards	Access, Amex, Diners, Visa
Bathrooms	Private showers (not WC) in rooms
Television	None
Breakfast	English
Telephone	Payphone
Parking	Plenty

The Coach and Horses is that rare phenomenon in London – a pub that is also a B&B. Charmingly situated right on Kew Green, this former coaching inn, parts of which date back to the 16th century, offers just six comfortable, newly-refurbished rooms.

On the ground floor is a cosy bar, popular with tourists and locals alike, and a restaurant. There are plans to turn the Coach and Horses into a much larger hotel, which might lose something of its charm but would please the many visitors who try to book in here without success.

Travel Instructions: *Underground to **Kew Gardens**. Turn right, down Station Avenue into Kew Gardens Road; turn left, then right at the main road. The Coach and Horses is on the far side of the green.*

Riverside Hotel

23 Petersham Road
Richmond
Surrey
TW10 6UH   Tel 081-940 1339

Price Band	££–£££
Credit Cards	Access, Visa
Bathrooms	Nearly all private
Television	In rooms
Breakfast	English
Telephone	In rooms
Parking	On street

From time to time one comes across a B&B that fulfills every criteria we looked for when researching this guide. Riverside does exactly that.

Set in a terrace of Victorian houses, one immediately notices the snowy-white drapes in the big bay windows and brass carriage-lamps flanking the front door. Inside is cosy and welcoming. Deep-pile, red carpet on the floor of the hall and stairways, bedrooms that are both comfortable and charming, some with river views and all with tea/coffee makers, and lovely bathrooms. The breakfast room is particularly attractive with windows both front and back (again views of the Thames), pink tablecloths matching the decor and fresh flowers adorning the tables.

Riverside is deservedly popular. Bookings should be made well in advance, especially for the rooms with a river view (no extra charge).

Travel Instructions: *Underground or train to* **Richmond.** *Turn left out of the station along the Quadrant which becomes George Street. Bear left into Hill Street which changes to Petersham Road after the bridge. Riverside is on the right. At least ten minutes' walk, so, with luggage, it is worth taking the 65 bus or a taxi. The romantically inclined can always take a boat as the hotel is situated directly above Richmond Pier!*

Kingston-upon-Thames

Kingston lies south of Richmond at the point where the winding River Thames flows northward in its journey to the sea. While lacking some of the charm of Richmond, it boasts pleasant riverside walks and a pier from where boats leave constantly, in summer, for many places of interest.

Now mainly a modern and thriving shopping and business centre, its chief claim to historical fame is the Coronation Stone, used to crown seven Saxon kings, which is preserved here.

Sports enthusiasts are well catered for with ice skating at Richmond, racing at Kempton and Sandown and tennis at Wimbledon all within easy reach. Although there is no underground here, central London is just twenty minutes by train via Waterloo and bus services are excellent.

Places to Visit

Bushey Park
Chessington World of Adventure
Hampton Court Palace and Park

Kingston Heritage Centre
Richmond
Wimbledon Lawn Tennis Museum

Pembroke Lodge
Guest House

35 Cranes Park
Surbiton
Surrey
KT5 8AB   Tel 081-390 0731

Price Band	£–££
Credit Cards	None
Bathrooms	Mainly shared – 3 rooms shower only
Television	In rooms
Breakfast	English
Telephone	Public
Parking	Plenty

What a delight when exploring the streets of Surbiton to come on this lovely B&B, one of those rare places which wins top marks on all counts: cleanliness, welcome, charm and value for money.

Spacious, comfortable bedrooms have attractive touches such as the cushions strewn on the beds which match the curtains. All are fitted with tea/coffee-makers and fridges while those at the back have lovely views of the garden and, in the distance, Hampton Court Palace.

However the outstanding feature of Pembroke Lodge is its elegant breakfast room which is worthy of a three-star hotel. Unusually situated on the first floor, pale green cloths cover the circular tables and a fine mahogany dresser supports a display of silver and crystal.

Disabled visitors are welcome here: a ground floor room has easy wheelchair access and breakfast can be served on a tray.

One cannot end this description without mentioning Scruples, the adorable labrador, who welcomes both human and doggy friends with the same enthusiasm.

Travel Instructions: *British Rail to Surbiton (15 minutes from Waterloo). Turn right up St Marks Hill and, after the main crossroads of Surbiton Hill Road, Cranes Park is the first left. Bus 71 linking Richmond, Kingston and Surbiton passes very nearby.*

Whitewalls Guest House

12 Lingfield Avenue
Kingston-upon-Thames
Surrey
KT1 2TN   Tel 081-546 2719

Price Band	£–££
Credit Cards	None
Bathrooms	Mainly shared, 3 private
Television	In rooms
Breakfast	English
Telephone	Payphone
Parking	Unrestricted on street

One is welcomed to the aptly named Whitewalls by the bright flower borders offsetting its gleaming facade and a friendly small dog who comes trotting to the door at the sound of the bell.

Inside is cosy and welcoming. Oak panelling in the public areas shows off a collection of bric-a-brac and bedrooms, all fitted with tea and coffee-makers, are spotless and comfortable.

Travel Instructions: *British Rail to Surbiton, turn right up St Marks Hill and left into Surbiton Hill Road. The third turning right, Beaufort Road, takes you into Lingfield Avenue – about ten minutes walk. Bus 71 passes the door and taxis are plentiful at both Kingston and Surbiton stations.*

Swiss Cottage

Swiss Cottage is predominantly a rich Jewish quarter with lots of shops, restaurants, banks etc. lying on the main Finchley Road and many quiet streets of elegant houses and pretty little gardens running off it on either side. Surprisingly, it is possible to find very reasonably priced holiday accommodation in the area and, since it is only ten minutes by tube from the centre, it is ideal for visitors who are looking for a safe and pleasant location to make their London base.

Places to Visit

Fenton House	Keat's House
Freud Museum	Kenwood House
Hampstead Heath	Regent's Park

Dawson House Hotel

72 Canfield Gardens
London
NW6 3ED   Tel 071-624 0079

Price Band	£
Credit Cards	None
Bathrooms	Shared
Television	In lounge
Breakfast	"Dutch" (see below)
Telephone	Public
Parking	Unrestricted on street

Lamps above the entrance posts, a pink rambling rose and a colourful striped canopy over the porch welcome visitors to Dawson House Hotel. Inside, the vision persists: all sorts of paintings cover the walls, a huge chandelier hangs from the ceiling of the lounge; shelves barely withstand the weight of numerous books; carpets are different not only from each other but also from those of other B&B's. There is stained glass in the hallway doors and intricate leaded-lights on the stairway. There is a bathroom on every floor. Bedrooms are plain and of course very quiet. Breakfast consists of cold ham and salami and four different types of cheese as well as the usual eggs, toast, etc.

Dawson House is without doubt one of London's top B&B's in its range and its prices are extremely competitive.

Travel Instructions: *Underground to **Finchley Road**. Turning right out of the station, you will find yourself already on Canfield Gardens. A 10-minute walk will take you to Dawson House, which is situated on the right. Drivers should note that this is a one-way street which must be approached from the Finchley Road end.*

Theydon Bois

Theydon Bois is a compact little 1930's village with a sprinkling of older pubs and houses. There are several restaurants, a bank and a selection of shops. For those travelling late at night, there is a minicab office immediately in front of the station.

Places to Visit

Epping Forest

Queen Elizabeth's Hunting Lodge

Parsonage Farm House ═══

Abridge Road
Theydon Bois
Epping
Essex
CM16 7NN   Tel 037-881 4242

Price Band	££–£££
Credit Cards	None
Bathrooms	Private and shared
Television	Available on request
Breakfast	English
Telephone	Use of house phone
Parking	Ample private parking

I came upon this delightful B&B quite by chance whilst out on a picnic one midsummer's evening. I was immediately struck by the fact that it stands in the heart of the Essex countryside whilst being only 10 minutes' walk from Theydon Bois Tube Station.

The house is a very attractive timber-framed building dating from the 15th century and faces livery stables across a courtyard. There are two acres of well-tended old-fashioned English gardens to the rear. Inside, furnishings are luxurious: deep, inviting sofas, antiques, beautiful china, etc.

Strongly recommended, not only for tourists who like to escape from the hustle and bustle of the city, but also for exhausted Londoners seeking a tranquil weekend retreat with exceptionally easy access: a direct journey of only 45 minutes on the Central Line will bring you from Oxford Circus to Theydon Bois.

Travel Instructions: *Underground to **Theydon Bois**. Turn left out of the station and cross the footbridge. Walking up a little lane with trees on either side, you will soon come into Abridge Road. The Parsonage Farm House is a few hundred yards further along on the left.*

If you are arriving by car, the farm is close to Exit 26 of the M25.

Wimbledon

Wimbledon is one of London's most pleasant suburbs, with acres of parkland and leafy residential areas where detached houses stand in large, well-manicured gardens. Residents still refer to the centre as the "Village" which, these days, is something of a misnomer as it is busy, thriving and congested with traffic.

For most people, however, the name Wimbledon means just one thing, for the name is synonymous the world over with lawn tennis and the famous championships that have been played here, every year, for over a hundred years. During those two weeks at the end of June/beginning of July, this quite ordinary suburb takes on a touch of magic. One meets few people who would not enjoy lazy summer days spent watching the play and eating delicious, though expensive, bowls of strawberries and cream. During the rest of the year one has to be content with visiting the on-site Lawn Tennis Museum with its attractive collection of tennis memorabilia (open Tuesday–Saturday and Sunday afternoons – admission charge).

Among the area's other attractions are one of London's few golf courses and two theatres; Wimbledon Theatre, built in 1910, stages pre-West End productions. The Polka Children's Theatre is open from Tuesday to Saturday for plays, puppet shows and exhibitions. Wimbledon has a good selection of restaurants, wine-bars and pubs, and public transport is good. Central London is just thirty-five minutes away by either underground (District line) or overground train. For motorists, parking is easy and places of interest such as Hampton Court, Windsor etc. are only a short drive away.

Places to Visit
Wimbledon Lawn Tennis Museum.

The Wimbledon Lawn Tennis Museum
See the famous Centre Court and Wimbledon Lawn Tennis Museum and Shop
Films are shown in the Museum Theatre
Open Tuesday to Saturday, 11am-5pm
Sundays 2pm-5pm
Closed Mondays and Bank Holidays
Admission £1.50 adults, 75p children & OAPs
Church Road, Wimbledon SW19 5AE
Telephone: 081-946 6131

Marple Cottage Guest House
113 Woodside
London
SW19 7BA   Tel 081-947 1487

Price Band	£
Credit Cards	None
Bathrooms	Shared
Television	In rooms
Breakfast	English
Telephone	Payphone
Parking	On street, free

Marple Cottage stands in a corner position and the Virginia creeper climbing up its walls and peeping in the bedroom windows gives a real "country" feel to this pleasant B&B, although owner Mrs McDermott says it is "taking over"! Spotless bedrooms have tea/coffee makers and several are large enough to accommodate en-suite facilities which are planned for next year. Many have an extra small bed, making this a good place for families. Children under 6 years stay free of charge.

Although slightly out of the town centre there is a convenient little row of shops right opposite which includes a pub and several restaurants.

Travel Instructions: *Train or underground to* **Wimbledon.** *Turn right out of the station and walk the length of Alexandra Road, turning left into Leopold Road. You will see the Marple Cottage on the corner of Woodside.*

Wimbledon Hotel ═══════

78 Worple Road
London
SW19 4HZ   Tel 081-946 9265

Price Band   £££
Credit Cards   *Access, Visa*

Bathrooms	*Mainly private*
Television	*In rooms*
Breakfast	*English*
Telephone	*In rooms*
Parking	*Plenty*

A solid red brick, double-fronted building, the Wimbledon Hotel is immediately warm and welcoming. Decorated throughout in light colours with an attractive blue carpet, it has a pleasant ground-floor lounge and breakfast room and spacious, comfortable bedrooms. All are fitted with tea/coffee makers, clock radios and lovely thick duvets on the beds. Especially good for families as children are very welcome and those under 8 years stay free of charge. Two ground floor rooms, opened during 1989, are ideal for disabled visitors and wheelchair access is possible to one – a spacious double.

Travel Instructions: *Train or underground to* **Wimbledon.** *Turn left into Wimbledon Hill Road, Worple Road is the second turning left and you will find the Hotel on the left. Many buses pass the door.*

AIRPORTS

Gatwick Airport

HORLEY

═══════════════════════════

Horley, a typical little country town, is just four minutes by train from Gatwick, London's second and fastest-growing airport.

Although Horley is in itself unremarkable, it has a number of excellent B&B's for the overnight visitor. Taxis to and from the airport are plentiful and cost about £2; journey time six or seven minutes.

For restaurants, the town has an Indian, a Chinese and a pizzeria, while motorists can drive to one of the large airport hotels for a drink and a meal. However, those in search of something special should take the ten-minute walk to Ye Olde Six Bells. Standing beside the river Mole, next to the 12th century St. Bartholomew's Church, this has been a pub for the last five hundred years, although its origins date back to AD857 when it was a retreat for the monks of Dorking Abbey.

Trains leave Victoria for Gatwick every 15 minutes from 6 a.m. to midnight – journey time half-an-hour; hourly trains during the night. Stopping services stop at Horley but these are much slower, so the best advice is use Gatwick station and take a taxi from there. There are frequent trains, also, to Brighton – locally known as "London by the sea" for its architecture and excellent hotels, shops, restaurants and entertainments.

The Cottage

33 Massetts Road
Horley
Surrey
RH6 7DQ   Tel 0293 775341

Price Band	£
Credit Cards	Access, Eurocard, Mastercard, Visa
Bathrooms	Public
Television	In rooms
Breakfast	Continental, served in rooms
Telephone	Payphone
Parking	Plenty

The Cottage is aptly named. A small and pretty black and white house, it has just five guest-rooms which, with their sloping ceilings and flower-sprigged bed linen, have a real country feel. Run by a friendly young mother, whose husband, an Italian, also speaks French and Spanish.

All rooms have tea/coffee making facilities, TV and radio alarms, and breakfast is served from 7 a.m. for early departures. Parking is free for guests who may also leave their cars here during holidays for £10 per week.

Travel Instructions: *From London, take British Rail to Gatwick, then taxi. Alternatively train to Horley. Walk down Victoria Road and Massetts Road is the second on the left.*

The Gables

50 Bonehurst Road
Horley
Surrey
RH6 8QG   Tel 0293 774553

Price Band	£
Credit Cards	None
Bathrooms	Mainly shared, 2 private
Television	In rooms
Breakfast	Continental
Telephone	Public
Parking	Plenty

The Gables is a calm and friendly B&B standing back from the main London-Brighton road (A23) in a large wooded garden. Its 22 rooms are double-glazed for quietness and absolutely shining as are the spacious bathrooms.

Travel Instructions: *Taxis to and from the airport cost £2.50, although guests departing before noon are given a lift in the owner's car. Otherwise from London by fast train to **Gatwick** or by stopping-train to **Horley**.*

Gainsborough Lodge ══════

39 Massetts Road
Horley
Surrey
RH6 7DI   Tel 0293 783982

Price Band	££
Credit Cards	Access, Visa
Bathrooms	Private
Television	In rooms
Breakfast	English
Telephone	Public
Parking	Plenty

The largest of the B&B's in leafy Massetts Road, Gainsborough Lodge is instantly recognisable by its attractive Dutch gable. From the pleasant reception area with its unusual brick desk and lots of useful tourist information on London, doors lead into the cosy little lounge and thence to the lovely breakfast room, furnished in pine with a rose-patterned ceiling and patio doors onto the garden.

Bedrooms are charming, all different and fitted with tea/coffee makers. Here the owner's good taste is very evident in the clever use of plain and patterned walls and interesting antiques, strategically placed. Gainsborough Lodge is a delightful B&B, and I was not surprised to learn that some guests cannot bear to leave and end up spending their entire holidays there!

Travel Instructions: *From London, British Rail to Gatwick then taxi. Alternatively train to Horley, walk down Victoria Road and Massetts Road is the second on the left.*

The Lawn Guest House ══════

30 Massetts Road
Horley
Surrey
RH6 7DQ   Tel 0293 775751

Price Band	£
Credit Cards	None
Bathrooms	Public
Television	In rooms
Breakfast	Continental
Telephone	Payphone
Parking	Plenty

One is welcomed to the Lawn Guest House by the friendly owners and their two adorable Golden Labrador dogs. Breakfast is served in the pleasant little dining room with its fresh blue and white china. The bedrooms have large windows overlooking the garden and are spacious enough to hold armchairs and coffee-tables as well as good-sized beds which are covered by pretty duvets. Alarm clocks are a useful extra.

Travel Instructions: *From London British Rail to Gatwick, then taxi. Alternatively train to Horley, walk down Victoria Road and Massetts Road is the second on the left. You will find the Lawn on your right.*

Rosemead Guest House ══════

19 Church Road
Horley
Surrey
RH6 7EY   Tel 0293-784965

Price Band	£
Credit Cards	None
Bathrooms	Public
Television	In rooms
Breakfast	English
Telephone	Payphone
Parking	Plenty

Another excellent B&B in an area, unlike Central London, where one is really spoilt for choice.

Working in close co-operation with the Lawn Guest House (page 00) Rosemead offers the same friendly welcome with hosts who have time for, and enjoy talking to, their guests; spacious, spotless bedrooms and pleasant public areas.

Children, and dogs, specially welcome.

Travel Instructions: *From London take British Rail to Gatwick then taxi. For motorists Church Road is a turning off the main A23, near the Chequers Hotel.*

Vulcan Lodge

27 Massetts Road
Horley
Surrey
RH6 7DQ   Tel 0293 771522

Price Band	££
Credit Cards	None
Bathrooms	3 private, 1 public
Television	In rooms
Breakfast	English
Telephone	Public
Parking	Plenty

Set a little back from Massetts Road, Vulcan Lodge is tiny but enchanting.

Consisting of only four rooms it is like a four-star hotel in miniature. Stripped pine floors are strewn with quality rugs and decor is in Laura Ashley style; flower-sprigged wallpaper, frilled window blinds and lovely original doors, again in stripped pine.

No expense has been spared to make Vulcan Lodge quite perfect, which it most certainly is. Highly recommended.

Travel Instructions: British Rail to **Gatwick** then taxi. Alternatively train to **Horley**, walk down Victoria Road and Massetts Road is the second on the left.

Heathrow Airport

HAYES and HOUNSLOW

Those wishing to be near Heathrow Airport for an early departure are advised to choose a B&B in either the Hayes or Hounslow area, since a tube journey of only ten minutes from Hounslow, or one by bus of the same duration from Hayes, will take them directly into the airport, while taxis from either cost a mere three or four pounds.

Both are typical London suburbs and have plenty of shops in their High Streets. Good transport facilities make other London tourism visits possible from this base and there are interesting attractions nearby. Kew Gardens, for example, are easily accessible from Hounslow.

Hounslow, especially, is a plane-spotters' paradise. Planes seem to take off or land every thirty seconds and are so low overhead that their every detail may be seen quite distinctly and the miracle of flight appreciated even more fully than when one is actually on board.

It only remains for us to wish you *Bon Voyage!*

Places to Visit
HOUNSLOW
Osterley House and Park
Syon House and Park
Hogarth's House, Chiswick

Musical Museum, Kew Bridge
Kew Bridge Steam Museum
Royal Botanic Gardens, Kew
HAYES
St Mary's Church

Bannon Rowe Hotel =========

293 Bath Road
Hounslow West
Middlesex
TW3 3DB   Tel 081-570 9072

Price Band	££
Credit Cards	None
Bathrooms	Shared; one family room only with private bathroom
Television	In rooms
Breakfast	English
Telephone	In rooms
Parking	Plenty, in forecourt

The Bannon Rowe is an unusual black and white building set back from the main road and dating from 1870. It has a series of cosy public areas – reception with easy chairs and sofa, sitting room, bar and dining room where evening meals as well as breakfast are served. Bedrooms are simple and pleasant and there is a garden available for the use of guests. Both the manager and her staff take a great interest in their guests and everybody may be sure of a warm welcome. Prices are approximately half of those charged by the modern airport hotels, making this lovely B&B a terrific bargain.

Travel Instructions: *Underground to* **Hounslow West.** *Turn left out of the station and you will find the Bannon Rowe on your left just two minutes' walk away.*

Fountain House

116 Church Road
Hayes
Middlesex
UB3 2LE   Tel 081-573 5453

Price Band	£££
Credit Cards	*Access, Visa*
Bathrooms	*Mainly private*
Television	*In rooms*
Breakfast	*English*
Telephone	*Public (see below)*
Parking	*Large car park*

The Fountain House, built in 1904, was originally a small public school, where the writer George Orwell (of "1984" fame), once taught, while the cottage in which he lived at the time is now used as an annexe. The latter, a much older building dating back to 1700, retains its original beams and is furnished in traditional style.

Rooms in both houses are cosy and comfortable with pleasing colour schemes, and facilities are excellent. There is a lift in the main building, also a bar and restaurant. Room telephones are planned but in the meantime one of the payphones is the most attractive I have seen – glassed-in and private, complete with armchair etc! Highly recommended, especially for motorists and those wishing to be near Heathrow.

Travel Instructions: *British Rail from Paddington to Hayes, then taxi (about £1.50) or bus 98. Taxis to the airport cost about £5 or, for those without much luggage, bus 140 passes nearby.*

Lynch's Guest House

123 Bulstrode Avenue
Hounslow
Middlesex
TW3 3AE   Tel 081-570 9343

Price Band	£
Credit Cards	*None*
Bathrooms	*Shared*
Television	*In rooms*
Breakfast	*English*
Telephone	*Public*
Parking	*Plenty, in forecourt or in street*

A top B&B in its category. The bedrooms are simple and pleasant and the dining room has French windows leading into a huge, well-tended garden which guests are encouraged to use. Run by a friendly, down-to-earth lady; it has far more the feel of a "family" B&B than some of those in the centre. Prices are amongst the most competitive in London.

Travel Instructions: *Underground to **Hounslow Central**. Turn left out of the station. Bulstrode Avenue is the first street on the right and Lynch's is half-way up on the right (five minutes' walk from the station).*

Special Requirements

To find the full entry for establishments included in the sections which follow, readers should cross-refer to the Index. There each B&B is listed alphabetically with a page number and also under its appropriate area.

Disabled Visitors

As stated in the introduction to this guide, no London B&B has been purpose-built. The majority have a flight of some six or so steps up to the front door and very few have lifts. Therefore they are unfortunately quite unsuitable for visitors with wheelchairs. However, there are a number which have either ground-floor bedrooms and breakfast-rooms and/or a lift and they may be suitable for people with less serious mobility problems. These include (the letter **C** = easy access by car):

Annandale		La Place	
Bedford Park	C	Lynch's	C
Central	C	Mitre House	C
Clearlake		Niki	
Concorde		Pembroke Lodge	C
Hamilton House		Plaza Continental	
Hindes Hotel	C	Regal	C
Holland Park		White House	C
Gables	C	Wimbledon	C
Gainsborough	C		

The Holiday Care Service is a charity which advises disabled people on accommodation in London. You may contact them at:

> 2 Old Bank Chambers
> Station Road
> Horley
> Surrey RH6 9HW
> *Tel:* 0293 774535

During the holidays only, the following university residence is also suitable for wheelchair access:

> Halliday Hall
> King's College
> 64-67 Clapham Common
> South Side
> London SW4 8AN
>
> *Tel:* 081-673 2032 (Price £)

Children

Children are welcome in most London B&B's, which usually prove a far happier environment, especially for little ones, than large, impersonal hotels. When taking children to a B&B it is a good idea to ask, at the time of booking, if any reductions are available. Also mention any special requirements such as a high chair or cot or babysitting. The latter, of course, is an extra and should be paid for accordingly.

Naturally the success of the visit depends very much on the parents, and an insistence on the same good behaviour they would expect in their own homes will certainly endear them to the proprietors. If damage or breakages do occur an offer of payment should always be made.

We have found the B&B's listed below to be particularly welcoming to children. You'll find the full entry by cross-referring to the Index.

Name of B&B	Area
Balmoral Hotel	Paddington
Bedford Park House Hotel	Chiswick

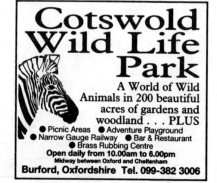

Camelot Hotel	Paddington
Centaur Hotel	Earls Court
Clearlake Hotel	Kensington
Edward Lear Hotel	Marble Arch
Europa House	Paddington
James House	Victoria
Kensbridge Hotel	South Kensington
Kenwood House	Marylebone
Marple Cottage	Wimbledon
Mr & Mrs Demetrious Guest House	Notting Hill
Melita House	Victoria
Mitre House	Paddington
Nayland Hotel	Paddington
Olympic House	Paddington
Parkwood Hotel	Marble Arch
Picton House	Paddington
Wimbledon Hotel	Wimbledon

Dogs

Those wishing to bring their dogs to London can encounter a number of problems, notably when travelling. The underground is often very crowded and most stations have escalators making their use impossible except for small dogs which can be carried. On buses dogs may travel on the upper deck but this is at the discretion of the driver/conductor which, in practice, is often not granted. Another problem is that most London B&B's, unlike their country counterparts, do not accept dogs.

However for those who have no alternative but to bring them or are showing their dogs at the famous Crufts show, the following will accept them, given prior notification. A wise precaution is to bring the dog's bed and a favourite toy to allay homesickness!

Name of B&B	Area
Bedford Park House Hotel	Chiswick
Brook Hotel	Chiswick
Mowbray Court	Earls Court
Pembroke Lodge Guest House	Kingston
Plaza Continental	Earls Court
Queensway Hotel	Paddington
Rosemead Guest House	Gatwick
Whitewalls Guest House	Kingston

Parking Facilities

As stated in the Introduction, parking in Central London is very difficult. It is also very expensive and anybody who parks illegally risks having their car clamped. Visitors coming to London by car are therefore strongly advised to stay at one of the B&B's listed below.

Name of B&B	Area
Arran Guest House	Ilford
Bannon Rowe	Heathrow (Hounslow)
Bedford Park	Chiswick
Bingham Hotel	Richmond
Brook Hotel	Chiswick
Centaur	Earls Court
Central Hotel	Harrow
Clevedun Hotel	Eltham
Coach & Horses	Kew
Conifers	Ilford
Cottage (The)	Gatwick (Horley)
Dawson House	Swiss Cottage
Edwards Guest House	Clapham
Elliot Hotel	Chiswick
Flaxman House	Chelsea
Fountain	Hayes (Heathrow)
Frognal Lodge	Hampstead
Gables (The)	Gatwick (Horley)
Gainsborough Lodge	Gatwick (Horley)
Hindes Hotel	Harrow
Lawn Guest House	Gatwick (Horley)
Lynch's Guest House	Heathrow (Hounslow)
Marlborough Hill	Harrow
Marple Cottage	Wimbledon
McCreadie Hotel	Forest Gate
Meadow Croft	Eltham
Mitre House	Paddington
Mrs Clements	Ealing
Olympic House	Paddington
Parsonage	Theydon Bois
Pembroke Lodge	Surbiton
Regal Guest House	Golders Green
Rhondda Guest House	Harrow
Rosemead Guest House	Gatwick (Horley)
St Peter's	Chiswick
Vulcan	Gatwick (Horley)
Weston	Eltham
White House	Ealing
Whitewalls	Kingston
Wimbledon Hotel	Wimbledon
Woodville Guest House	Ilford
Yardley Court	Eltham
York	Ilford

Classified Index

ENTERTAINMENT

Bond Street Tickets, 114 Bond Street, London W1 (071-935 8116). Concerts, shows, sporting events. You phone, we deliver the tickets.

Canal Cafe Theatre, Bridge House, Delamere Terrace, Little Venice W2 9NG (071-289 6054). Theatre and Restaurant. The best of food and entertainment.

Open All Hours (071-379 4444). Credit card booking for theatre, concerts and sport. 24 hours, 7 days a week.

Premier Box Office Ltd., 188 Shaftesbury Avenue WC2 (071-240 2245/0771). Send SAE for full Theatre Guide and Pop Concert List.

FAMILY HISTORY & HERALDRY

Achievements Ltd., Centre for Heraldic and Genealogical Research, Northgate, Canterbury, Kent CT1 18AB (0227 462618). Write for free estimate.

GETTING AROUND

Holiday Payless Car Rental (UK) Ltd., PO Box 127, Crawley, Sussex RH10 4GZ (0293 785772). Low cost car hire. No hidden extras.

MUSEUMS & GALLERIES

Bank of England Museum, Threadneedle Street EC2R 8AH (071-601 5898). Traces the Bank's history from 1694. Exhibits and inter-active videos.

Dulwich Picture Gallery, College Road SE21 7BG (081-693 8000). Collection of Old Masters in building designed by Sir John Soane.

Florence Nightingale Museum, 2 Lambeth Palace Road SE1 7EW (071-620 0374). Life and work of the pioneer of modern nursing.

The Guards Museum, Wellington Barracks, Birdcage Walk SW1E 6HQ (071-930 4466 ext. 3271). The story of the five Regiments over 300 years.

Kingston Heritage Centre, Wheatfield Way, Kingston-upon-Thames, Surrey KT1 2PS (081-546 5386). Exhibition of the work of Eadweard Muybridge, pioneer of cinematography.

Museum of the Moving Image, South Bank SE1 8XT (071-401 2636). The world's most exciting cinema and television museum.

Pitshanger Manor Museum, Mattock Lane, Ealing W5 (081-567 1227 or 081-579 2424 ext. 42683). Georgian and Regency rooms. Martinware pottery. Occasional Art Exhibitions.

Shakespeare Globe Museum, Bear Gardens, Bankside, Southwark SE1 9EB (071-620 0202). Shakespeare and theatrical history.

Wimbledon Lawn Tennis Museum, All England Club, Church Road, Wimbledon SW19 5AE (081-946 6131). The history of lawn tennis.

RESTAURANTS

Beefeater Steak Houses. Great value at Handsel Tavern, 5/6 Argyll Street W1 (071-437 1143) and St. Martin's Tavern, John Adam Street WC2 (071-839 2697).

Bombay Palace, 50 Connaught Street W2 2AA (071-723 8855). Authentic North Indian cooking. Daily buffet lunch.

City Limits, Wake Arms Roundabout, Epping High Road, Essex CM16 5HW (037-881 2618). Restaurant-bar in excellent out-of-town location. Ideal for any occasion.

Entrecote. Downstairs at 124 Southampton Row, London WC1 (071-405 1466/8640). Lunches and Dinners with Dancing. Open seven days.

SHOPPING

Australian Gift Shop, Western Australia House WC2R 0AA (071-836 2292). Australian goods, books, food. Aussie dollar Gift Vouchers.

The Best of British, 27 Shorts Gardens, Covent Garden WC2 (071-379 4097). A wide range of individually crafted items from throughout the British Isles.

Peter Dale Ltd., 11 & 12 Royal Opera Arcade, Pall Mall, London SW1 4UY (071-930 3695). Fine antique arms and armour for the collector.

Gift Flair, 15 and 67 Buckingham Palace Road SW1 (071-834 8729/071-828 7703). All kinds of London souvenirs. Open 7 days 9a.m. to 8p.m.

TOURS & VISITS

Catamaran Cruisers Ltd., Charing Cross Pier, Victoria Embankment, London WC2N 2NU (071-839 3572). Cruises, floating restaurant, disco, etc.

Cotswold Wildlife Park, Burford, Oxfordshire (099-382 3006). A world of wild animals. Open daily 10am to 6pm.

Discover Islington, the REAL London. At home atmosphere and rich heritage. Information from Clerkenwell Heritage Centre, 33 St. John's Square EC1M 4DN (071-250 1039).

Flying Scotsman Services (0524 734220). Steam-hauled train journeys on B.R.! For details of our all-day tours please telephone (Monday to Friday 9am to 5pm).

Guinness World of Records, The Trocadero, Piccadilly W1V 7FD (071-439 7331). Over 20,000 facts and feats brought to life. Open daily 10am to 10pm.

London's Docklands. Where the past meets the future. An exciting mixture no visitor should miss. Phone (071-222 1234) for travel information.

Perfect London Walks, PO Box 1708 NW6 1PQ (071-435 6413). From Pub Crawls to Ghost Hunts – 17 different walks each week. No pre-booking necessary.

Royal Britain Exhibition, opposite Barbican Tube (071-588 0588). Experience the spectacular story of Britain's monarchy.

Thames Barrier Visitors Centre, Unity Way, Woolwich SE18 5NJ (081-854 1373). The largest moveable flood barrier in the world – without this attraction you might not see the rest.

Tobacco Dock, Pennington Street, Wapping. Quality shops, pirate ships, restaurants, entertainment. Open 7 days a week.

Hotel Index

Abbey House, *Kensington High Street* 39
Adare House, *Paddington* 57
Albany Hotel, *Bloomsbury* 19
Albro House, *Paddington* 57
Allandale, *Paddington* 57
Amsterdam Hotel, *Earls Court* 35
Annandale House, *Chelsea & Sloane Square* 30
Arran Guest House, *Ilford & Forest Gate* 92
Astors, *Victoria* 67

Badger House, *Chiswick* 77
Balmoral Hotel, *Paddington* 59
Bannon Rowe Hotel, *Heathrow Airport* 106
Bedford Park House, *Chiswick* 77
Bingham Hotel, *Kew & Richmond* 95, 96
Brook Hotel, *Chiswick* **76**, 78

Camelot Hotel, *Paddington* 59, **60**
Cartref House, *Victoria* 67
Cavendish Hotel, *Bloomsbury* 22
Centaur Hotel, *Earls Court* 35
Central Hotel, *Harrow* 90
Chesham House Hotel, *Victoria* 68

Clearlake Hotel, *Kensington High Street* 40
Clements, Mrs J.A., *Ealing* 82
Clevedun Hotel, *Eltham* 84
Coach and Horses, *Kew & Richmond* 96
Collin House, *Victoria* **67**, 68
Concord Hotel, *Earls Court* 35, 36
Concorde Hotel, *Marylebone & Marble Arch* 49
Conifers Guest House, *Ilford & Forest Gate* 93
The Cottage, *Gatwick Airport & Horley* 103
Crescent Hotel, *Bloomsbury* 19

Dawson House Hotel, *Swiss Cottage* 99
Demetriou's Guest House, *Notting Hill & Holland Park* 54
Dylan Hotel, *Paddington* 59

Eaton House, *Victoria* 68
Ebury House, *Victoria* 69
Edwards Guest House, *Clapham* 81
Edward Lear Hotel, *Marylebone & Marble Arch* 48
Elizabeth Hotel, *Victoria* 69

Elliott (Private) Hotel, *Chiswick*   78
Enrico Hotel, *Victoria*   70
Euro Hotel, *Bloomsbury*   20
Europa House, *Paddington*   **56**, 60

Fielding Hotel, *Covent Garden*   33
Fouberts, *Chiswick*   79
Fountain House, *Heathrow Airport*   107
Frognal Lodge Hotel, *Hampstead & Golders
    Green*   87

The Gables, *Gatwick Airport & Horley*   103
Gainsborough Lodge, *Gatwick Airport &
    Horley*   104
Garden Court Hotel, *Bayswater*   15
Garth Hotel, *Bloomsbury*   20, **25**
George Hotel, *Bloomsbury*   20
Golders Green Hotel, *Hampstead & Golders
    Green*   87
Gower House Hotel, *Bloomsbury*   21

Haddon Hall Hotel, *Bloomsbury*   21
Hallam Hotel, *Marylebone & Marble
    Arch*   49
Hamilton House, *Victoria*   70
Hampstead Village Guest House, *Hampstead &
    Golders Green*   88
Harcourt House, *Victoria*   70
Harlingford Hotel, *Bloomsbury*   **20**, 21
Hart House, *Marylebone & Marble Arch*   49
Henley House, *Earls Court*   36
Hindes Hotel, *Harrow*   90
Holland Park Hotel, *Notting Hill & Holland
    Park*   54
Hotel 167, *Knightsbridge & South
    Kensington*   43
Hotel Cavendish, *Bloomsbury*   22
Hotel Concorde, *Marylebone & Marble
    Arch*   49
Hotel La Place, *Marylebone & Marble
    Arch*   50, **51**
Hotel Plaza Continental, *Earls Court*   37

Ivanhoe Suites, *Marylebone & Marble
    Arch*   50
James House, *Victoria*   71
Jenkins Hotel, *Bloomsbury*   22, **25**
Jesmond Hotel, *Bloomsbury*   23

Kensbridge Hotel, *Knightsbridge & South
    Kensington*   44
Kenwood House, *Marylebone & Marble
    Arch*   51
The Knightsbridge, *Knightsbridge & South
    Kensington*   44

La Gaffe, *Hampstead & Golders Green*   88,
    89
La Place Hotel, *Marylebone & Marble
    Arch*   50, **51**
The Lawn Guest House, *Gatwick Airport &
    Horley*   104
Lewis House, *Victoria*   71
Lynch's Guest House, *Heathrow Airport*   107

Mabledon Court Hotel, *Bloomsbury*   23
Manzis, *Soho*   64
Marlborough Hill Guest House, *Harrow*   91
Marple Cottage Guest House,
    Wimbledon   101

McCreadie Hotel, *Ilford & Forest Gate*   93
Meadow Croft Lodge, *Eltham*   84
Melita House, *Victoria*   71
Mentone Hotel, *Bloomsbury*   24
Mitre House, *Paddington*   **58**, 60
Moderna House, *Paddington*   61
Morgan Guest House, *Victoria*   72
Morgan Hotel, *Bloomsbury*   24
Mowbray Court Hotel, *Earls Court*   37

Nayland Hotel, *Paddington*   **58**, 61
Niki Hotel, *Paddington*   61

Observatory House Hotel, *Kensington High
    Street*   40
Olympic House Hotel, *Paddington*   **56**, 72
Olympic House Hotel, *Victoria*   62

Parkwood Hotel, *Marylebone & Marble
    Arch*   **48**, 51
Parsonage Farm House, *Theydon Bois*   100
Pembroke Lodge Guest House, *Kingston-upon-
    Thames*   98
Picton House Hotel, *Paddington*   62
Plaza Continental Hotel, *Earls Court*   37
Pyms Hotel, *Victoria*   72

Queensway Hotel, *Paddington*   62

Regal Guest House, *Hampstead & Golders
    Green*   89
Rhondda Guest House, *Harrow*   91
Richmond House Hotel, *Victoria*   **67**, 73
Ridgemount Private Hotel, *Bloomsbury*   25
Riverside Hotel, *Kew & Richmond*   96
Rosemead Guest House, *Gatwick Airport &
    Horley*   104
Royal Oak, *Bayswater*   16
Ruskin Hotel, *Bloomsbury*   26
Russell House Hotel, *Bloomsbury*   26

St. Margarets Hotel, *Bloomsbury*   **25**, 26
St. Peters Hotel, *Chiswick*   **77**, 79
Searcys Roof Garden Rooms, *Kinightsbridge &
    South Kensington*   44
Sir Gar House, *Victoria*   73
Swiss House Hotel, *Knightsbridge & South
    Kensington*   **43**, 45

Terstan Hotel, *Earls Court*   37
Thanet Hotel, *Bloomsbury*   **20**, 27

Vicarage Private Hotel, *Kensington High
    Street*   41
Vulcan Lodge, *Gatwick Airport &
    Horley*   **11**, 105

Wansbeck Hotel, *Bloomsbury*   28
Westminster House Hotel, *Victoria*   74
Weston House, *Eltham*   85
White House, *Ealing*   82
Whitewalls Guest House, *Kingston-upon-
    Thames*   98
Wimbledon Hotel, *Wimbledon*   102
Windermere Hotel, *Victoria*   74
Woodville Guest House, *Ilford & Forest
    Gate*   94

Yardley Court, *Eltham*   85
York Hotel, *Ilford & Forest Gate*   **92**, 94